"IN THE COUNTRY OF THE ENEMY"

New Perspectives on the History of the South series provides a forum for the best new
scholarship on the ever-changing South. It emphasizes books that focus on the
region's social, economic, cultural, and intellectual history, especially those with an
interdisciplinary emphasis. Its goal is to ask fresh questions about the South and to
provide stimulating answers, arguments that in turn add to the on-going dialogue
of historical analysis about that ever-fascinating land.

"In the Country of the Enemy": The Civil War Reports of a Massachusetts Corporal,
edited with an introduction by William C. Harris

"In the Country of the Enemy"

THE CIVIL WAR REPORTS
OF A MASSACHUSETTS CORPORAL

Edited by William C. Harris

FOREWORD BY JOHN DAVID SMITH

UNIVERSITY PRESS OF FLORIDA
Gainesville · Tallahassee · Tampa · Boca Raton
Pensacola · Orlando · Miami · Jacksonville

04 03 02 01 00 99 6 5 4 3 2 1

LIBRARY OF CONGRESS CATALOGING-IN-PUBLICATION DATA

Haines, Zenas T., 1830–1900.
In the country of the enemy: the Civil War reports of a Massachusetts Corporal / edited with
   an introduction by William C. Harris; foreword by John David Smith.
p. cm. — (New perspectives on the history of the South series)
Articles written by newspaperman Zenas T. Haines under the pseudonym "Corporal" which
   were first published in the Boston Herald and subsequently published in book form.
Originally published: Letters from the Forty-fourth Regiment M.V.M.A. Boston: Printed
   at the Herald Job Office, 1863.
Includes bibliographical references (p.) and index.
ISBN 0-8130-1678-9 (cloth: alk. paper)
1. North Carolina—History—Civil War, 1861–1865—Personal narratives. 2. United States—
   History—Civil War, 1861–1865—Personal narratives. 3. Haines, Zenas T., 1830–1900. 4.
   United States. Army. Massachusetts Infantry Regiment, 44th (1862–1863). 5. Journalists—
   Massachusetts—Boston—Biography. 6. Soldiers—Massachusetts—Biography. I. Harris,
   William C. (William Charles), 1933–. II. Haines, Zenas T., 1830–1900. Letters from the
   Forty-fourth Regiment M.V.M.A. III. Title. IV. Series.
E524.H35 1999
973.7'44—dc21   98-48012

The University Press of Florida is the scholarly publishing agency for the State University
System of Florida, comprising Florida A&M University, Florida Atlantic University, Florida
International University, Florida State University, University of Central Florida, University of
Florida, University of North Florida, University of South Florida, and University of West
Florida.

University Press of Florida
15 Northwest 15th Street
Gainesville, FL 32611
http://www.upf.com

For
Corinne, William, Stephen, Rachel, and Euclid

CONTENTS

ILLUSTRATIONS

FOREWORD

The Civil War shaped the South's identity as much as any other single event in the region's rich history. Ironically, though white Southerners seceded from the Union determined to chart a course separate and apart from Northerners, the armed conflict brought thousands of Yankees to Dixie to suppress what President Abraham Lincoln described as "an insurrection against the Government of the United States."

Zenas T. Haines (1830–1900), a veteran newspaperman from Maine who wrote for the *Boston Herald,* was just one of thousands of Northerners who came south during the war and recorded his impressions of Southerners white and black. In the first contribution to New Perspectives on the History of the South, William C. Harris of North Carolina State University, one of the nation's leading authorities on the Civil War and Reconstruction, has ably edited and introduced Haines's valuable collection of firsthand observations of war-torn eastern North Carolina.

Haines, who signed his letters "Corporal," published them originally in the *Herald* in 1862–63. They provide an insightful documentary record of almost eight months of U.S. military service in North Carolina's swampy lowlands. Haines's nine-month regiment, the 44th Massachusetts Volunteer Militia, was organized in August 1862 and served until its discharge in June 1863. The 44th consisted largely of well-educated, middle-class Bostonians—students, clerks, lawyers, and businessmen. The men generally defined the Civil War idealistically as a crusade, first and foremost to save the republic from the South's treason. It was, as Haines explained, a "glorious contest for the integrity of our country." Though Haines was no abolitionist (he in fact subscribed to the common white racial stereotypes of his day), the journalist nonetheless opposed slavery and sympathized with the slaves he encountered in North Carolina. He wrote favorably of blacks who served as spies for the U.S. Army and endorsed the recruitment and mobilization of emancipated slaves as armed soldiers. In Haines's opinion, the men of the 44th were following God's will to purify the South by "the fire and the sword." He missed few opportunities to compare the hated "secesh" unfavorably with what he considered the more progressive yeomen of New England.

Corporal Haines's letters emphasize the rigors of military service from the perspective of the common soldier. While he was careful not to criticize his superiors openly in print, Haines nevertheless noted the privileges accorded those who wore shoulder straps, not stripes. After a treacherous trip south by sea to the North Carolina coast in which many of the enlisted men succumbed to seasickness, the 44th joined the large Union military base in New Bern, North Carolina. The regiment fought in three campaigns: in Tarboro in November 1862, in Goldsboro in December 1862, and in the Confederate siege of Little Washington in April 1863.

Haines's letters are among the richest descriptions of U.S. military operations in eastern North Carolina, including critical commentary on Union troops as stragglers and looters. In addition to his narrative of the 44th's military engagements, students of social history will value Haines's detailed descriptions of mundane soldier life: jealousies between regiments, camp morals, diversions, and amusements. Haines noted not only the soldiers' 1862 celebrations of Thanksgiving and Christmas in New Bern, but also the folk traditions and rituals of the freedpeople who sought refuge behind Union lines.

Thanks to Professor Harris's labors, a broad audience now will be able to read Haines's insightful comments on the Civil War in eastern North Carolina. In clear and precise prose, the journalist underscored the seriousness and pathos of war, the contradictory emotions of citizen soldiers far away from home engaged in a holy but frightful war. Proud of his regiment and proud of his cause, Haines articulated well the zeal of men willing to sacrifice their lives to squelch the slaveholders' rebellion and to keep the Union intact.

John David Smith

EDITORIAL METHOD

In editing this work, I have followed closely the 1863 published compilation of Haines's reports by the *Boston Herald* Job Office. The 1863 printing reflects a careful attention by Haines, aided perhaps by the *Herald* editor, to literary style and clarity. A copy of the original publication, titled *Letters from the Forty-Fourth Regiment M.V.M.: A Record of the Experience of a Nine Months' Regiment in the Department of North Carolina in 1862–3. By "Corporal,"* can be found in the North Carolina Collection, University of North Carolina at Chapel Hill.

A few editorial changes have been made. I have standardized the print, indentations, and spacing of the lines and also noted spelling errors, which are few. No attempt was made to modernize the spelling. I have also provided in square brackets the given names of persons identified only by their last names in Haines's reports. In a few cases, the first names of men in other regiments and Massachusetts civilians have not been found. I have annotated information on individuals, organizations, places, events, literary allusions, and obscure and anachronistic references to food and other items.

Valuable information on the men of Haines's regiment appears as a tabular roster in *Record of the Service of the Forty-Fourth Massachusetts*

Volunteer Militia in North Carolina, August 1862 to May 1863 (Boston: Privately printed, 1887), 302–35. Compiled by veterans of the regiment during the 1880s, this roster provides the name of each member of the regiment, his rank, company, age at enlistment, where enlisted, last known residence, and last known occupation. A final column in the roster provides brief information on the individual after his service in the 44th regiment.

ACKNOWLEDGMENTS

Several individuals and institutions have assisted me in the preparation of this book. My two graduate assistants, Nancy Kaiser and Mike Smith, have aided in the research on Zenas T. Haines and his comrades in eastern North Carolina. Ann Baker Ward and her staff of the Interlibrary Loan section, D. H. Hill Library, North Carolina State University have contributed immensely to the procurement of source materials that assisted me in writing the Introduction and identifying the many references to people, places, and events that Haines mentioned in his reports to the *Boston Herald.* The staffs of the North Carolina State Library, Raleigh, the Southern Historical and North Carolina Collections, University of North Carolina at Chapel Hill, the Perkins Library, Duke University, have also provided materials for the study.

Specific research information has been generously provided by Sion Harrington III of the North Carolina Division of Archives and History; Walter B. Hill, Jr., of the National Archives, College Park, Maryland; Virginia H. Smith of the Massachusetts Historical Society; Karyl S. Perry of the Center for Maine History, Portland, Maine; Gerald W. Thomas of Laurel, Maryland; and Carl Robin of Fairfield, Pennsylvania. Photographs for the book have been graciously supplied by Michael J. Winey of the U.S. Army Military History Institute, Carlisle Barracks, Pennsylvania; and Richard Shrader of the Southern Historical Collection, University of North Carolina at Chapel Hill. Assistance has also been provided by John M. Riddle of the Department of History, North Carolina State University.

I am enormously grateful to Norene Miller for typing the manuscript and performing other tasks associated with the production of the book. Finally, I want to thank my colleague John David Smith, the general editor of this series, for his careful reading of the manuscript and his thoughtful suggestions for changes. I owe a great deal to Professor Smith for his interest in this project and in my other scholarly endeavors.

INTRODUCTION

On August 4, 1862, the War Department in Washington issued a call on the governors for 300,000 nine-month militias to fill an immediate need for troops after General George B. McClellan's costly failure to take Richmond. An effort earlier in the summer to raise a similar number of three-year volunteers had faltered as the columns in Northern newspapers groaned with long casualty lists from the South. Under a congressional act of July 17, 1862, authorizing the enrollment of nine-month state troops, the War Department could draft the necessary men, if a state did not meet its quota. Known as the Militia Act, this measure marked the first step toward national conscription in the North. Congress, in order to placate sensitive governors, particularly Governor John A. Andrew of Massachusetts, and at the same time encourage militia volunteers, agreed to give each recruit a month's advanced pay when his company was fully organized. The act also encouraged communities to pay enlistment bonuses or bounties to their nine-month militia volunteers.[1] This provision ultimately led to the notorious bounty system that, while providing monetary incentives for recruits, became riddled with corruption and injustice.

Satisfied that the states could recruit, organize, and select regimental officers under the Federal militia enactment, Governor Andrew moved quickly to raise his state's quota of 19,090 volunteers. Massachusetts communities, but not the state, offered bonuses (the average amount per man was slightly more than $100), and when enrollments lagged in the Boston area, local authorities drafted 520 men to fill the ranks. By the end of the year 16,685 nine-month volunteers had been raised in the state and organized into seventeen infantry regiments.[2] Though Massachusetts did not completely fill its quota, the War Department, which had questioned the value of enrolling men for such a brief period of time, made no effort to obtain the full complement of nine-month troops from the state. In 1863 the department secured a Federal system of conscription and volunteering to replace the decentralized and unfair system of state control of recruitment. Most of Massachusetts' nine-month troops would serve in North Carolina under General John G. Foster and in Louisiana under General Nathaniel P. Banks.

One nine-month recruit was Zenas T. Haines (1830–1900), a native of Maine and a newspaperman with the *Boston Herald,* a moderate Democratic daily that vigorously supported the war. Haines joined the 44th Massachusetts Volunteer Militia Regiment and served in North Carolina as a corporal in Company D. He wrote a series of articles or reports for the *Herald* vividly describing the military life of the troops, beginning with the regiment's organization in August 1862, then its garrison and combat service in North Carolina, and concluding with its homecoming in June 1863. The articles, written under the pseudonym *Corporal* and subsequently published in book form by the *Herald,* provide an intelligent and often humorous history of a Union regiment from the perspective of a journalist serving in the ranks. Though Haines on one occasion alluded to the censorship of correspondence pertaining to military intelligence, he never suggested that any part of his reports was ever excised by authorities. The standard bibliography on Civil War publications refers to the Haines book as "the most comprehensive account by a private soldier of the 1862–1863 campaigns in North Carolina."[3]

Haines's articles also describe the attitudes of New England soldiers toward the war, opinions regarding their officers, camp life, and conditions in eastern North Carolina where the war took a cruel toll on civilians of both races. Haines often contrasted life in "rebeldom" with the refined society that he knew in New England. Though not an ardent abolitionist, Haines, like many fellow New England Democrats as well as Republicans, opposed slavery. Haines applauded Lincoln's Emancipation Proclamation and, despite occasionally repeating racial stereotypes in his reports, he developed a great deal of sympathy and admiration for blacks. He especially came to respect the former slaves for their valuable support as spies and soldiers for the Union military cause in eastern North Carolina.

Unfortunately we know little about Corporal Haines before and after his service in the 44th regiment. A thirty-year-old newspaper editor in Strong, Maine, at the outbreak of the war, by 1862 Haines had moved to Boston, where he worked for the *Herald*. On May 26, 1862, Haines joined the 4th Battalion of Infantry, Massachusetts Militia, a state force organized by Governor Andrew for three-months' duty in the South. The next day, however, Haines, along with other enrollees, was deactivated after the War Department telegraphed Andrew that it could not accept the battalion for such a brief period of service.[4] When the order for nine-month troops was issued in August, the governor called the 4th Battalion to active duty and made it the nucleus for the organization of the 44th Volunteer Militia Regiment. Haines joined Company D, one of ten companies in the regiment, and on August 29 reported to camp at Readville, near Boston.[5] The next day, Haines began his series of articles for the *Boston Herald* on life in the 44th Massachusetts.

The 44th regiment, consisting of approximately ninety-eight enlisted men in each company, was remarkable for its demographic distinctiveness. Most of the men were young professionals, clerks, and college students from the Boston area; some represented the cream of the city's society. Haines provides a statistical profile of the enlisted men in two of the companies, including his own (pages 58–59, 62–63). In his company, Haines identified fifty-four former clerks, five merchants, and nine students of Tufts, Harvard, and Yale. One member of the company was the well-known Harvard astronomer Horace Parnell Tuttle, who, reportedly out of patriotic zeal, volunteered after rejecting an attractive offer of a position at the National Observatory in Washington.[6] For the remaining enlisted men in his company, Haines noted an assortment of occupations and professions. However, he identified only four as farmers, seven as skilled workers, and none as common laborers.[7] Calculating the average age in his company at twenty-two, Haines indicated that ninety of the men were unmarried. Though only seven men indicated that they were abolitionists, sixty-one identified themselves as antislavery Republicans, which typified the political affiliations of Massachusetts voters.[8] Of the remainder, thirteen referred to themselves as Democrats and thirteen as "Union men," presumably independents who opposed an antislavery purpose in the war. Haines did not reveal his own political identity, though he probably was an antislavery Democrat. Whatever his earlier views of slavery, Haines during the period of his military service in North Carolina developed a strong dislike for the South's "peculiar institution" as he observed firsthand its pernicious and degrading features. In contrast, his editor (and proprietor) at the *Boston Herald,* though proclaiming slavery "a curse," opposed Lincoln's emancipation policy on the grounds that it would divide the North and cause the South to fight harder.[9]

Unitarians and Universalists dominated Haines's data on religious affiliations, with sixty-three men listed as members of these two liberal denominations. Haines was a Universalist, his father, Peter, having been one of the founders of the denomination in Maine.[10] Interestingly in view of Massachusetts' strong Congregational heritage, only thirteen indicated membership in the "Orthodox" church. The statistics for F Company, as copied by Haines from the *Boston Advertiser,* reflected a similar profile.

Though not bedrock Calvinists, the young men of the 44th regiment subscribed to the Puritan ideal that every person was his brother's keeper.

They exuded the spirit of moral reform that, they believed, was essential to the maintenance of the good society at home and the preservation of the republic and its institutions and liberties in the country at large. In going south, men of the 44th carried these values with them and inevitably compared Southern society unfavorably with their own in Massachusetts. For example, in a Thanksgiving Day address in the barracks in North Carolina, A. L. Butler of Company F reminded his comrades of the reasons for New England's progress, contrasting that region with the benighted and oppressive South. "Much of the success and prosperity of New England of to-day can be traced to the principles, habits, and institutions that our forefathers practiced and established," Butler declared. "Success is inscribed on the Yankee character; and whatever the Yankees attempt to perform, that will they accomplish, [including] the suppression of the Southern rebellion." Butler asked: "What man among us, during our late march through a portion of this State, could help contrasting the want of industry, prosperity, and intelligence, with the neatness, thrift, and happiness of a New England village?"[11] Three weeks later Butler died in the battle of Whitehall for the cause that he espoused.

But first the men of the 44th regiment had to prepare for war, with training designed to develop the closeness, discipline, and skill that were so essential for soldiers in enemy country and under enemy fire. Encamped at Readville from late August to late October 1862, they underwent the usual military drilling, marching, learning about their equipment, firing their rifle muskets, and performing camp details.[12] They proudly claimed that the professional men and clerks in the regiment, despite a contrary belief, proved more able to endure the hardships of military life than the outdoorsmen in the regiment. The training exercises were new and difficult for the recruits; otherwise, the transition from civilian to military life at Readville generally proved pleasant. The regimental officers, who were respected citizens of Boston and vicinity and who, in most cases, had served in militia organizations, including their commander Colonel Francis L. Lee, quickly gained the respect of the troops.[13] Though Corporal Haines in his reports to the *Herald* naturally avoided criticizing his superiors, his comments and those of diarist Corporal John J. Wyeth clearly suggest genuine affection for most of the regiment's officers.[14]

At first the officers did not apply rigid military discipline. Instead, they placed a great deal of emphasis on instilling unit pride in the troops, or inspiring what modern military men term "small-unit cohesion." The officers of the 44th encouraged company competition on the parade ground, on the firing range, and in the policing of the barracks. Discipline, however, tightened as the training period advanced and the time approached for the regiment's departure to the war zone.

Local Massachusetts citizens, like many Northern civilians elsewhere, viewed themselves as participants in the war. They provided material and moral support for the troops in camp at Readville and even after they went south. The people of Boston and vicinity showered the men with attention, clothes, food, and money for medical and other supplies. Hardly had the soldiers settled into their barracks, when civilian friends and relatives descended upon the camp, bringing with them wine, fruit, pastries, tobacco, cigars, and an assortment of practical items, including tailor-made uniforms. Perhaps with some exaggeration, the *Boston Herald* reported on September 17 that thousands of people had visited the camp the preceding day. Dress parades, with music sometimes supplied by the Boston Brass Band, attracted Massachusetts dignitaries and, more important for the troops, young women who took the train from the city. Haines understated when he reported: "the number of pretty girls that adorn these occasions, coming as they do, laden with offerings of fruits and flowers for their favorites, is by no means the least interesting feature of the afternoon [parades]" (p. 49). On long marches through nearby towns, "beautiful women" smiled and waved handkerchiefs as the men passed, inspiring the men to greater military ardor.

Though it could not compare with the allurements of the opposite sex, music provided a major form of diversion for the men of the 44th at Readville and later in North Carolina. Each company had a choir, and one company had its own band that accompanied the singers and played for dances. James B. Gardner, a member of Haines's company, recalled that "scarcely an evening passed during our whole term of service without a gathering of the choir, and the performers were always sure of a sympathetic and appreciative audience." Several talented members of the regiment composed songs for the troops, and Private Charles C. Ewer, also of Haines's company, compiled and had published a collection of this music.[15]

One form of diversion that Colonel Lee did not tolerate was the consumption of alcohol, except for wine in small amounts or as prescribed by surgeons. Temperance reform had swept New England during the 1850s, and Colonel Lee, as well as many of his troops, believed that strong liquor had no place in an army of moral virtue and discipline. The colonel waged a relentless and largely successful campaign against "traffickers in the ardent," who attempted to establish clandestine booths near the camp.[16] Colonel Lee also proved no friend of tobacco. He ordered his troops not to smoke in the barracks, a command that was frequently honored in the breech. In addition, the colonel was no friend of those who used profanity; he forced the resignation of a lieutenant whose language was "more forcible than elegant" in dressing down an enlisted man.[17]

Finally, on October 2, the 44th and two other nine-month Massachusetts regiments received orders to embark for New Bern, North Carolina, as soon as transport ships could be made available.[18] Most of the troops, with typical recruit bravado, hailed the news that at last they would be leaving to strike a blow against the rebellion and for the glory of New England and the Union. They realized that their carefree life as recruits would end once they sailed from Boston for the hostile South.

When the 44th arrived in Boston to board the steamer *Merrimac* for the voyage to North Carolina, the citizens turned out to give the troops a rousing Godspeed. Since the regiment, consisting of 1,018 enlisted men and officers, was mainly from the Boston area, the send-off was no ordinary affair. The *Boston Traveller* of October 22 provided an account of the 44th regiment's bittersweet farewell. Forming ranks on Boylston Street, the regiment marched to the Boston Common where a large crowd of well-wishers greeted them, and where the men said their good-byes to families and friends. Then, accompanied by a band and escorted by a platoon of police and aging members of the New England Guard, the 44th passed through the downtown streets to the waves and cheers of thousands of Bostonians. Many in the throng followed them to the wharf, where the ship waited.[19]

A rude awakening greeted the troops of the 44th when they boarded the *Merrimac*. As Haines reported, the men of his company were "packed like so many herrings in the steerage," with little more than space to turn over in their bunks. Others were not as fortunate; they had to sleep on the cold deck, upon the hatches, in the passage ways, and wherever they could find a resting place (p. 69). The officers, however, had cabin accommodations and food that was far more appetizing than the bread and boiled beef and potatoes served to the enlisted men. Though Haines was careful in his dispatches to the *Herald* not to cast aspersions on the regimental officers, the tone of his account of the voyage suggested that many of the men, whose level of education, social standing, and age were similar, resented the special treatment that the officers received. Equality, however, existed in one form: seasickness. Despite pleasant weather, on the second day at sea, nausea struck both officers and men. Below deck, fresh air and salubrious living conditions existed at a premium. Haines ruefully reported that "a prison dungeon is not worse supplied with air and sunlight" than the quarters on the *Merrimac* (p. 71). Fear also swept the ship when a report circulated that the notorious Confederate raider *Alabama* could be seen on the horizon. As soon revealed, the ship was another troop transport heading south, but concern continued, since no provision had been made for an armed escort for the *Merrimac*.[20]

After a three-day voyage, the troops arrived at Morehead City, North Carolina, a small port near Beaufort Inlet that had railroad connections with New Bern. Transported to New Bern on open cars in a driving rain, a distance of forty-two miles, the men of the 44th received a depressing view of the eastern North Carolina countryside, an area that had been tenuously occupied by Federal forces since the spring. Haines and others

Eastern North Carolina during the Civil War. Reproduced from Charles Dana and E. Kay Gibson, *Assault and Logistics: Union Army Coastal and River Operations 1861–1866.* The Army's Navy Series, Volume II. Camden, Maine: Ensign Press, 1995.

in his regiment wrote home describing in unflattering terms the terrain and the people of this region of North Carolina. Their initial impression did not appreciably improve during the regiment's seven and one-half months in the state. Haines wrote after arriving in New Bern that "a more miserable and worthless tract of country than the barren pine region which we traversed cannot well be imagined." Reporting that the troops "witnessed several good specimens of the real Southern 'white trash'," Haines ungenerously remarked that "the country is well calculated to develop this species of the genus homo. The women are the most doleful and disgusting looking of their sex. We suspected all of them of looking secesh daggers at us" (p. 75). Henry Austin Clapp of Company F reported that he "saw a few of the 'poor white trash' at the doors of their miserable houses, always with flocks of children." He believed that all of the white people, including women and children, were seceshs; most of the men were in the rebel army. John Wyeth, also of Company F, concluded that "North Carolina was a tough place, barren and desolate, and hardly worth the cost of fighting for."[21]

The troops of the 44th also had their first contact with blacks, whose masters either had fled with the approach of the Federal army or remained at a safe distance from the picket posts along the railroad. Blacks probably had learned of President Lincoln's preliminary Emancipation Proclamation (September 22, 1862) from the antislavery New Englanders manning the posts. Believing that the troops came as liberators, they smiled and waved as the 44th passed their "huts." When the train stopped, blacks sold the soldiers sweet potatoes, the only crop that seemed to grow in the swampy pine country of coastal North Carolina.[22]

Arriving at their destination on October 26, the men of the 44th found New Bern a welcome relief from their hard trip and the depressing scenes that they had witnessed along the railroad. Strategically located at the confluence of the Neuse and Trent rivers, New Bern since its fall to General Ambrose E. Burnside's army in March 1862 had become the center for Federal forces in eastern North Carolina. Here Federal troops, supported by navy gunboats, had launched military operations along the waterways of the Pamlico and Albemarle region of the northeastern part of the state. Although they had occupied and fortified such river towns as Elizabeth City, Plymouth, and Washington and conducted brief raids into the immediate vicinity, Union forces had not attained their chief objective of seizing the Wilmington and Weldon Railroad.[23] This railroad, which by the fall of 1862 had become a major supply line for Robert E. Lee's army in Virginia, was arguably the best protected railroad in the South. Furthermore, the lowland terrain in eastern North Carolina made it difficult for a Federal army to move quickly against a point on the railroad before a sizeable Confederate force could be rushed to its defense.

When General Foster replaced General Burnside in command of the Department of North Carolina in July, he pleaded with the War Department to send sufficient reinforcements to North Carolina that would enable him to launch a large-scale operation against the railroad at Goldsboro.[24] The success of this campaign, Foster argued, could be followed by a direct assault on Wilmington and the forts at the mouth of the Cape Fear. The War Department partially responded to Foster's appeal by dispatching the nine-month Massachusetts troops and other volunteer units to New Bern. With the arrival of the nine-month regiments in late October, the strength of Union forces in North Carolina stood at 15,569. The figure would rise to more than 20,000 by the time that Foster was ready to launch his campaign against Goldsboro.[25]

Upon arrival, the 44th Massachusetts regiment was assigned to the Second Brigade commanded by Colonel Thomas G. Stevenson and including four other New England regiments, one of which along with the 44th was a nine-month unit. On December 28 the Department of North Carolina was organized as the Eighteenth Army Corps, commanded by Foster, with a division under the command of Brigadier General Henry W. Wessells and three unattached brigades. The corps also included five artillery batteries, a cavalry regiment, and a detached brigade from the Fourth Army Corps stationed in Virginia. In the reorganization, the 44th Massachusetts continued in Stevenson's brigade, which was placed in Wessells's division. A reorganization of the Eighteenth Army Corps occurred in March 1863 when the Second Brigade, including the 44th Massachusetts, was detached to the Fourth Division, temporarily commanded by Colonel T. F. Lehmann. The 44th ended its service in North Carolina as one of several regiments in two "independent brigades" in the First Division commanded by Brigadier General Innis N. Palmer.[26]

The New Bern that the 44th regiment came to was an armed camp that included thousands of troops, earthen fortifications protecting the land approaches, and numerous gunboats and steamers on the mile-wide Neuse River. In addition to its seemingly impregnable defenses, the men of the 44th found much to appreciate about the town. A prosperous commercial center before the war and North Carolina's second largest town with a population of more than 6,000, New Bern possessed wide streets, running at right angles and shaded by large hardwood trees. Though not of the classical Greek revival associated with the Old South, attractive houses with broad verandas and luxuriant gardens immediately brought to the minds of the New England troops the homes and communities they had left. Indeed, some of the men referred to New Bern as "the New Haven of the South." Abandoned by their owners upon the approach of the Union army, the elegant homes of New Bern's merchant and professional class were now occupied by Federal officers. New Bern also had five churches for whites, two for blacks, an academy, several public buildings, a theatre, two first-class hotels, and a newspaper, edited by a sergeant selected for the task by General Burnside.[27] In addition, Military Governor Edward Stanly, whom Lincoln had sent to North Carolina to establish the nucleus of a Union government in the state, had his headquarters in New Bern. By 1863 Stanly, whose proslavery and conservative sentiments did not sit well with Haines and other antislavery troops, had failed in his mission and had left North Carolina. Lincoln did not replace him.[28]

New Bern also had attracted hundreds of blacks escaping the hard hand of slavery and war. Vincent Colyer, appointed by General Burnside as superintendent of the poor for occupied eastern North Carolina, by the summer of 1862 estimated that there were 7,500 "contrabands" (blacks) in the New Bern area. This figure would grow after Lincoln's Emancipation

Proclamation, and, though several hundred blacks had joined the Union army and were sent elsewhere, this number had increased to more than 8,500 by January 1864. These refugees from slavery provided the troops with inexpensive delicacies, such as cakes and pies, labor, and services. Several hundred blacks were employed, if not conscripted, to build fortifications at New Bern and other coastal points. Burnside directed that they be paid eight dollars a month and given one ration a day and clothing.[29] Though New England soldiers generally approved of Lincoln's Emancipation Proclamation, many held antiblack sentiments. One Maine soldier reflected the antiblack view of many New England troops in eastern North Carolina when he wrote that slavery "is wrong, a curse," but that he "could not bear" the sight of blacks. Along with others in General Foster's army, this soldier favored emancipation as a war measure, designed primarily to weaken the Confederacy and only secondarily as an act of humanity for the slaves. Such men did not hesitate to exploit black refugees, forcing them to work as servants for little compensation.[30] Haines, while believing in white superiority, did not engage in blatantly racist actions or language.

Hardly had the men of the 44th Massachusetts regiment settled into their "splendid new barracks" and explored the town when they received orders to embark by steamer for Washington, North Carolina, where the Tar River flowed into the Pamlico River. As was usually the case with the troops in the ranks, they could only speculate about the purpose of the movement.

Using Washington as a base, General Foster, who personally commanded the operation, planned to march on Tarboro, hoping to capture three enemy regiments foraging in the area and threatening Federal forces at Plymouth and elsewhere in the Albemarle region. This campaign would be preparatory to a major assault farther south on Goldsboro in December. Arriving at Washington on October 31, the 44th regiment, along with other units, on November 2 began the overland movement toward Tarboro, a distance of more than fifty miles. Six miles from Williamston, the Federal troops, totaling about 5,000 men,[31] encountered a rebel force of 700 or 800 fortified in rifle pits and behind hastily constructed field works. In the ensuing two-hour fight, the 44th Massachusetts, only seven weeks after its mustering into the Union army and one week after its arrival in North Carolina, received its baptism of fire. Foster's force greatly outnumbered the rebel defenders and succeeded fairly easily in driving them from their positions. The 44th regiment, as a part of the vanguard brigade in what became known as the battle of Rawle's Mill, performed well and lost only two dead and seven wounded. Corporal Haines exulted in the role that his regiment had played in scattering the rebels, writing that after the battle the 44th "gain[ed] expressions of admiration from the old regiments in the expedition, who had previously regarded . . . us as more ornamental than useful."[32] Military men have long known that the first experience of neophyte troops under fire is the most dreaded and uncertain; at Rawle's Mill the 44th regiment passed this important test of "moral endurance and pluck." The men were now confident that in more serious engagements with the rebels they would bring greater honor and glory to themselves and the Union.

The Tarboro expedition, however, did not provide them with another opportunity to demonstrate their battlefield courage and effectiveness. After Rawle's Mill, Foster's forces became mired in a difficult and frustrating march through enemy territory, encountering only light armed resistance but accomplishing little militarily. This area of North Carolina was an important agricultural region, and the men lived off the land, seizing corn, hogs, horses, poultry, and other products from farms and plantations, many of which had been abandoned by their owners upon the approach of Foster's army. The moral code of some New England troops did not prevent them from plundering civilian homes. Outright pillaging of household goods and the wanton destruction of property occurred, an ominous foretaste of the Federal army's hard war on the South during the last half of the conflict. Near Hamilton, a Confederate picket's attack on a Union soldier became the excuse for troops to set fire to several buildings in the town. The flames quickly engulfed nearby residences and led to wholesale pillaging of homes and businesses. Upset by the conduct of these soldiers, Haines assured his readers back home that the incendiary actions of the few "was generally condemned as unnecessary and outrageous" (p. 86). However, he did not condemn those who had plundered the town. For New England soldiers like Haines, who disdained if not hated Southern rebels, the line between the legitimate seizing of provisions and the pillaging of homes and businesses became blurred as they marched and raided through hostile country. Haines found such foraging incidents, bordering on outright thievery, "among the amusing episodes of our progress through North Carolina" (p. 89).

Unlike soldiers in other wars and some in the Civil War armies, the New England troops in North Carolina rarely, if ever, assaulted noncombatants. Attacks on women and children, unless in self-defense, outrageously violated their high moral code. Despite the bitter and open hostility of Southern white "hell-cats" toward them, these troops, including those who never professed traditional Puritan ideals, understood the severity of their punishment if they crossed the line and assaulted women. Years later, the historian of the 44th Massachusetts and a veteran of the regiment sought to assuage any guilt regarding the Federal burning and looting of Hamilton. He took pains to explain to his readers that "our boys refrained from such unsoldierly conduct [as pillaging], and, beyond searching for and securing articles and animals for food, they respected the property of the citizens."[33]

Leaving Hamilton in flames, the Federal troops marched westward through swampy country toward Tarboro. While encamped in rain and mud about ten miles from Tarboro, General Foster learned that the enemy had been substantially reinforced and was preparing to take the offensive against the Federals. With his troops exhausted (many were sick) and short on provisions, Foster ordered a rapid retreat back to Hamilton. There Union gunboats provided supplies and cover from an anticipated Confederate attack that never occurred. Regaining their strength at Williamston, Foster's troops made a quick march of twenty miles to Federal-occupied Plymouth on the Roanoke River, where they embarked on steamers and schooners for the return to New Bern. In writing about the results of the operation, Haines expressed pride in his regiment's performance, having marched successfully about one hundred miles through hostile and difficult country and with only a few stragglers. The march, Haines quaintly concluded, had "taught us something of the wonderful endurance and elasticity of the human frame, which rusts out through the enervation of idleness and vicious habits faster than it wears out by the sturdy hardships of the soldier" (p. 96). He believed that the expedition had "succeeded in cleaning the rebel troops out of a large part of North Carolina, and in giving them a terrible scare" (p. 88).

General Foster, on the other hand, concluded that the Tarboro operation had accomplished only one object: it had prevented a rebel attack upon the strategic Federal position at Plymouth.[34] Even this success was suspect, since one month later, in December, Confederate raiders seized Plymouth and burned half the town before retiring in the face of a counterattack by Federal gunboats. As would be the case in all Federal operations into rebel territory after Lincoln's Emancipation Proclamation, Foster's forces freed a large number of slaves—several hundred by one count—who followed the army to Plymouth and other Union-occupied river towns.[35] Haines wrote that bringing freedom to blacks provided an "inspiration to us" and a hope that the rebellion would soon be crushed (p. 88).

Back in New Bern, the men of the 44th Massachusetts rested, recounted tales of the Tarboro campaign, caught up on their correspondence and reading, and settled into the routine of camp life. Units in both the Federal and Confederate armies, including the 44th regiment, made the most of their respites from combat operations. Troops of the 44th, consisting of an unusually large number of educated and creative men, endeavored during their stay at New Bern to replicate as much as possible the life that they had known in Massachusetts. Thanksgiving Day, occurring two weeks after their return from the Tarboro excursion, provided soldiers of the 44th, along with other New England troops, with an opportunity to celebrate their region's most important holiday. When military duties permitted, men of the 44th made painstaking preparations for a magnificent Thanksgiving celebration. General Foster, himself a New Englander, cooperated by declaring Thanksgiving Day (November 27) a holiday for all the Federal troops in the Department of North Carolina and directed that military drills not be conducted on that day.

In his account describing the events of the day, Haines remarked that Thanksgiving "[c]ould not have been observed with more feeling and *eclat* by the same individuals at home." The troops, joined by Military Governor Stanly and army officers, "dined luxuriously," listened to speeches, played music, danced, and attended "literary" performances in the barracks (p. 98).[36] As with soldiers in all wars, home was not far from the thoughts of the men of the 44th during the holiday. Haines wishfully concluded his account of Thanksgiving in North Carolina with the hope "God grant that the next [one] may be in New England, and for new and more important reasons than has yet impelled us to perpetuate the example of the Pilgrims." He meant the complete triumph of the Union and the end of human bondage in America.

After Thanksgiving, preparations for the next military campaign intensified. Corporal John J. Wyeth of Company F confided to his diary on December 9 that "drill, drill, drilling" characterized every waking moment as the men prepared for an unknown destination into enemy territory. "We would hardly be recognized [now] as the same boys who have occupied the barracks since Thanksgiving night," he wrote.[37]

On December 11 the troops marched out of New Bern and headed toward Kinston, beginning the largest Federal campaign in North Carolina until near the end of the war. Their objective was the important Wilmington and Weldon Railroad. Led by General Foster and consisting of approximately 11,000 men, the army planned to sever the railroad at Goldsboro, about sixty miles from New Bern. Marching through largely swampy and wooded terrain, the Federals' first important encounter with the Confederates occurred at Southwest Creek, twenty-nine miles from New Bern. Though in the line of battle, the 44th Massachusetts, in what became known as the battle of Kinston, participated only as skirmishers in the successful Federal assault to take the bridge over the creek. Kinston now fell to Foster's army, and the 44th regiment encamped on the outskirts of the town. Haines and his comrades witnessed an event in Kinston that became all too familiar when Federal troops captured a town—the firing of cotton bales by retreating Confederates and the looting by troops and others before order could be restored.[38]

The next day the Federal army continued its movement toward Goldsboro. After a long, forced march of fifteen miles on a sandy road, the 44th Massachusetts bivouacked in a cornfield near the Neuse River. The following morning Foster's army reached Whitehall, a small river village, where they found the bridge over the Neuse destroyed and Confederate troops in a strong position on the other side. As part of the vanguard brigade, Haines and his comrades were ordered to move forward to the banks of the Neuse and engage the rebels. When they did, the 44th immediately came under a withering fire, forcing them to seek protection behind a rail fence. After more than an hour in this precarious position and suffering several casualties, the 44th retreated. Haines and his comrades made it to safety "by hugging mother earth and folding our arms back of our heads." They crawled with "bullets whistling close to us in a neighborly fashion." A battery of Federal artillery, supported by the 44th riflemen, soon silenced the rebel fire except for a few sharpshooters.[39]

Instead of crossing the Neuse, the Federal troops resumed their march south of the river, eight miles from the Wilmington and Weldon Railroad bridge below Goldsboro. Arriving at the bridge the next day, December 17, Foster's vanguard encountered a determined Confederate force. After a fierce fight, with the 44th Massachusetts held in reserve, the Federal troops took the bridge and set it ablaze. The troops in reserve had agonizing moments to engage in simple diversion. While waiting for an order to enter the fray, Haines and his comrades made a "lively charge" upon "a mound of sweet potatoes between us and the enemy" (p. 113). Persuaded that the bridge had been destroyed and learning that Confederate troops from Virginia and South Carolina were hurrying to save the railroad, General Foster, without doing further damage to the roadbed or entering

Goldsboro, ordered a retreat to New Bern and abandoned the second part of his plan, a campaign against Wilmington. As soon revealed, damage to the line was only superficial, and in a few days trains were running again across it.[40]

Foster's army, exhausted and "chawed-up," returned to New Bern on December 20. One soldier wrote that he was so tired when he reached camp that he had "no distinct idea of those last seven miles" of the march, "except that he was trying to walk, smoke, and go to sleep at the same time."[41] General Foster, however, extravagantly claimed that the "expedition was a perfect success," since his forces had defeated the enemy in four engagements and had burned the Wilmington and Weldon Railroad bridge.[42] Corporal Haines did not share this rosy view of the Goldsboro campaign.[43] Still, Haines was careful not to report a setback for Federal arms in North Carolina lest it contribute further to the demoralization at home after General Burnside's disastrous defeat at Fredericksburg on December 13. In his account of the operation, the "Corporal" lashed out at the stragglers on the march and the "white-livered wretches who fall out of the ranks at the first bidding of the cannon's voice" (p. 109). He also complained that many of the soldiers had loose tongues, which provided the rebels with important information, particularly intelligence of a Federal shortage of ammunition and supplies.

Though he praised the leadership and courage of his officers, particularly Colonel Francis L. Lee, the 44th commander, Haines's confidence in the rank-and-file soldier had suffered, but not that in his own regiment. Haines doubted that Foster's troops generally "are as brave and patriotic as the average" soldier. The Federal army in North Carolina, Haines believed, had lost something of its élan as a result of the Goldsboro campaign. But then, as historians have noted, failure to achieve their military objective, whether admitted or not, will cause most soldiers to despair and blame other units of the army for the lack of success. When reports appeared in Boston "reflecting upon the bravery" of the 44th, Haines angrily answered in the Boston Herald. The reason for the "malicious falsehoods," he declared, was because men of "the old regiments from Massachusetts," who received no bonuses when they joined the army, "will never forgive us because we were voted bounties *after* we had enlisted" (p. 116).

For soldiers like Haines, the regiment was the central institution in their military lives. As historian Earl J. Hess has written, it provided special, mutually supportive relationships that transcended explanation. As in the case of the 44th, members of the regiment were residents of the same town or area and had joined the army in response to community sentiment and support. "Once in uniform, they forged bonds of trust and affection that went far beyond civilian acquaintances," Hess writes. The experience of hard marches across difficult terrain and in all types of weather knitted the regiment into a band of brothers that could endure the ultimate test of the soldier on the battlefield.[44] This tight community of men reached maturity in the 44th Massachusetts in the Goldsboro campaign. Troops from all of Massachusetts' nine-month regiments in North Carolina, however, could agree with Haines that no one "desires a repetition of these little excursions of Gen. Foster," and each man would "give his nine months' pay and bounty for the certainty of serving his country as well by remaining at Newburn [*sic*] during the rest of his term of service" (p. 109).

Haines's experience in two combat operations caused him to question whether Northern correspondents in reporting the bravado of the soldiers going into battle were really telling the truth, an issue that modern scholars have also raised. "The man who says he loves to face the 'leaden rain and iron hail' of battle is either a liar or a monstrosity," Haines wrote. "No man who cares for life and friends can go into battle without a natural shudder and dread. The wonder is that duty and pride are strong enough in any man to urge him forward into the very teeth of death." Haines, true to his view of the war as a crusade, told his readers that "the soldier who unmurmuringly meets and performs his duties of hardship and danger must be provided with something of that divine armor which fits him to be a soldier of the cross" (p. 109).

Preparations for the Christmas and New Year season in New Bern soon gave Haines and his comrades the opportunity to forget their humiliating retreat from the outskirts of Goldsboro. In the same report to the *Herald,* written on January 2, lamenting his disappointment with the army's performance, Haines gave an extended account of the holiday festivities in camp. Like troops in this and other wars, the highlight of the season for the "boys" of the 44th was the arrival of "the bounties and luxuries of home." The men experienced the spirit of Christmas by decorating the barracks and arranging for musical and dramatic entertainment. The performances of "contraband," or black dancers and minstrels, added to the enjoyment of the troops. Visitors from home, including officers' families, also enlivened the season.

The men of the 44th Massachusetts continued throughout January to find musical and theatrical programs lively diversions from their camp duties and relief from their anxieties regarding the next military operation. These activities also provided them with the opportunity to avoid the winter monotony and boredom that afflicted soldiers in less talented and educated regiments. On January 20, in Haines's barracks, the troops held the "first grand Terpsichorean festival of the New Year." The parts of the "feminine element," "Corporal" reported, were performed by "young men with smooth faces and an eye to artistic effect" (p. 118). A "Grand Ball," attended also by Colonel Lee and the regimental staff, provided the climax for the night's entertainment. Haines noted the sharp contrast between such revelry and the hard reality of war that awaited the men at any moment. "It affords the two emotional extremes," he wrote. "One day finds [the soldier] in the midst of hilarity and social enjoyment, the next in the blood and carnage of battle, with friends falling all about him" (p. 122).

An outbreak of malaria, occurring during the unlikely month of January, brought another hard reality of war to the camp. Before the epidemic had run its course, eight members of the 44th regiment had died and many others had contracted the fever. Reporting to his readers that malaria did not usually occur after the first frost, Haines blamed the late outbreak to a severe drought that "so reduced the bulk of the water in the neighboring swamps as to leave a margin of mud, which has sent forth the fever poison" (p. 122). Sadly, he had come close to the truth of the cause, the mosquito that hatched in the mud. The army surgeons prescribed daily dosages of quinine to prevent the fever; amazingly, in view of the consequences for failure to take the medicine, some of the men refused it until ordered to do so.[45]

After six weeks of inactivity, on January 31 the 44th Massachusetts received orders to embark on the transport steamer *Northerner* for Plymouth on the Roanoke River. The movement was part of a series of winter operations ordered by General Foster to check Confederate encroachments on Federal outposts in eastern North Carolina that were preparatory to a spring campaign against New Bern and other Union-controlled areas. Plymouth, protected by gunboats, was the key to the upper Roanoke Valley, a fertile region that provided badly needed grain and meat for Robert E. Lee's army in Virginia and Confederate forces in North Carolina.[46]

When Colonel Francis L. Lee, along with his regiment, arrived at Plymouth, he assumed control of the small Federal garrison there. Lee immediately began preparations to advance on Williamston, about twenty miles upriver where Confederates reportedly were concentrating. A dispute with Lieutenant Commander Charles W. Flusser, commander of the gunboats at Plymouth, over the objectives of the expedition and the extent of naval support for the operation caused Colonel Lee to change his plans and remain in Plymouth. A snowstorm also contributed to Lee's decision to abandon the operation. Flusser was furious. He virtually charged the commander of the 44th Massachusetts with cowardice and asked Lee "if his men came out here to fight or to eat Uncle Sam's grub."[47]

Actually, Flusser, whose gunboats had an easy time controlling the waterways, underestimated the supply problems facing the neophyte army troops in an operation through the swamps of the area. Even during their brief stay at Plymouth, the men of the 44th had to forage for their "grub." Colonel Lee went out on the Washington road with several of his companies, including Haines's unit, to sweep the area for food and dry wood. A cold, overnight march took them through swamps, as well as agricultural lands, and, after a twenty-five-mile trek, they returned with provisions for a few days. Having apparently deterred the small Confederate buildup in the area by their presence at Plymouth, and with their transport steamer, the *Northerner,* running short on coal, the 44th regiment on February 8 embarked for New Bern.[48]

After returning to camp, barracks details, drills, parades, and preparations for a "Grand Masquerade Ball" on George Washington's birthday occupied the time of the 44th Massachusetts men.[49] A great deal of work, in which Haines was involved, went into the arrangements for the ball. The affair, attended by Generals Foster and Henry W. Wessells, the division commander, and officers from various regiments at New Bern "crowned and surpassed all [their] previous efforts in this line," according to Haines, who devoted most of two articles to an account of it. No doubt the festivities, including the usual comedy skits, organized by Haines and his comrades, provided entertainment for a large number of young men who still were civilians at heart and separated, for the first time in many cases, from family and community. Such activities as balls and theatrical programs for Massachusetts men who generally shunned alcoholic beverages, cards, and low night-life provided a delightful and even exciting diversion.[50] (Interestingly, in view of their popularity among the New England troops, Haines, a Universalist, did not comment on religious services in the regiments, though he reported that the New Bern churches were crowded with soldiers on Sundays.)[51] General Foster and his officers did not miss the point that these activities boosted morale throughout the camp during the winter months, always a difficult period for an army awaiting the resumption of fighting in the spring.

The spring military campaign came early in eastern North Carolina. On March 14, the day General Foster had scheduled a grand review of the troops to celebrate the first anniversary of the Federal occupation of New Bern, Confederates, under the overall command of General Daniel

Harvey Hill, launched a three-pronged attack on the Union defenses near the town. The planned review of the army never occurred. Pushed back at first, the Federal outposts held until Union gunboats could get into position and shell the attacking Confederates. The Confederates, with only light batteries to contest the gunboats on the Neuse and under heavy artillery fire from the shore, had to retreat.[52] Except to send out pickets, after the rebels had "skedaddled," the 44th Massachusetts did not participate in the action. Haines reported that the troops "[were] not much frightened" by the attack. He boasted that "the rebels will always find Newbern a hot place" (p. 140). His assessment proved accurate. Two subsequent Confederate attempts, both in 1864, failed to breech the formidable Federal defenses.

Failing to take the Federal stronghold at New Bern, General Hill sent his forces against Little Washington with the purpose of expelling the enemy from the Tar–Pamlico River area. General Foster at first could only guess where the next attack by the Confederates would come. Not realizing that a major rebel effort would be made against Washington, Foster ordered the 44th Massachusetts, except for two companies, to reinforce the small garrison there. On the morning of March 16, with only two hours' notice, Haines and his comrades departed New Bern "with no idea of a longer stay than ten days' rations implied." The troops brought no change of clothes and only blankets to keep them warm at night. Colonel Lee complained to Foster's headquarters that "in this condition we are extremely uncomfortable, and the men will soon become sick on account of unavoidable filth." He asked that the regiment be recalled as soon as Washington was safe from a Confederate attack.[53] It would be more than a month before Lee's request for redeployment to New Bern could be honored.

The 44th arrived at Washington in the evening of the 20th to an enthusiastic reception by the garrison troops and "contrabands who came [down] to the river in flocks" to greet the men. For the first time in North Carolina, soldiers of the 44th were ordered to raise their tents.

Acting independently of the division and brigade commanders, who remained at New Bern, and following General Foster's instructions, Colonel Lee assumed command of all of the forces at Washington. These men numbered about 1,200 and included two companies of the 1st North Carolina Union Volunteers. Colonel Lee also armed a body of former slaves, probably the first blacks recruited in the Federal army in North Carolina.[54] Within a few days, Haines reported that "our colored recruits are already winning golden opinions for their soldierly qualities. Our most bitter negropholists admit that they will fight." He marveled that "some of the poor fellows lie behind the breastworks with a spelling book in one hand and a musket in the other" (p. 154). In addition to the military forces in Fort Washington, as the post was called, three navy gunboats lay anchored in the river and prepared to aid the troops. Fortunately for the Federals, they had several days to perfect their defenses before Hill's forces arrived.

Meanwhile, General Foster had learned of General Hill's movement toward Washington and on March 30, along with his staff, rushed to the scene, evading the Confederate guns at Hill's Point that now dominated the entrance to the river. Foster also left orders in New Bern for the dispatch of an overland expedition to reinforce the Fort Washington defenders. The relief force, consisting of 6,400 troops and led by General Francis B. Spinola, the least experienced of the three brigadiers left at New Bern, never reached its destination. It was defeated at Blount's Creek, midway between New Bern and Washington, by a smaller force under the command of General James Johnston Pettigrew. Spinola's broken army "skedaddled" back to New Bern, tarrying long enough to fell trees to cover its retreat. Foster, assuming command from Colonel Lee, frantically strengthened the town's defenses and sent out units to scout and harass the Confederate army that was converging on Washington.[55]

After viewing the strong enemy fortifications, General Hill decided to clamp a siege on Fort Washington and let his artillery pound the Federals into submission, a suggestion that Generals Robert E. Lee and James

Longstreet had made to him in order to avoid heavy losses. Throughout early April, Confederate batteries around Washington bombarded the Union blockhouses, breastworks, and small makeshift earthen forts or bomb-proofs. The Federal troops and gunboats responded in kind, and General Foster sent out pickets to man outposts as a trip wire in case of a rebel infantry assault on the fort's perimeter.[56] Because of the effectiveness of the defenses, the Confederate bombardment caused only light Federal casualties; and no important infantry attack occurred on the fortifications.

Though his reports to the *Herald* could not be sent at the time, Haines wrote an almost daily account of the siege. His reports from Washington, especially, revealed confidence in the Union defense and also a growing appreciation for the ordeal experienced by blacks in the area and the support that they were giving to the Union cause. Haines also expressed sympathy for "poor white people who had been left behind here" and who were victims of the rebellion that they supported. He was appalled by the high rate of illiteracy among the whites and by the backwardness of the area's society. The "Corporal" wrote that "even those of respectable appearance, [were] unable to read or write." Like many of his idealistic New England comrades, Haines concluded that "the more we learn of the despicable social condition of the South, the stronger appears the need of the purification which, in the Providence of God, comes of the fire and the sword" (p. 149).

On April 14, under cover of darkness, the steamer *Escort* with the 5th Rhode Island regiment and provisions on board ran the Confederate batteries and effectively ended the siege. General Hill realized that the arrival of Federal reinforcements and supplies made the capture of Fort Washington unlikely. He slowly withdrew his men, to the cheers of the Union troops and blacks who had endured the sixteen-day siege against an enemy force of approximately 9,000.[57] After the Goldsboro fiasco, General Foster's success at Washington restored troop morale in North Carolina and provided a small but welcome boost to the Union cause in the North, occurring soon after the winter of the Federal army's failures in Virginia.

It also offered a crucial breathing period for Federal forces in eastern North Carolina. Not until early 1864, after the departure of the nine-month troops, did the Confederates launch another major offensive to retake the area; this effort also failed. Along with other Federal units at Washington, the 44th Massachusetts volunteers received the praises of northeastern newspapers for their stand during the siege. Haines could hardly contain his pride when he wrote that General Foster, the hero of the siege, remarked that the 44th had performed better than any other nine-month regiment in the army (p. 162).

"Having contributed to the salvation of Little Washington," Haines and his comrades returned to New Bern on April 24. They were immediately assigned provost-guard duty, an assignment that continued for the remainder of their service in North Carolina. Haines found police duty "severe, irksome, and often abhorrent" and expressed the hope that the regiment's "reputation as policemen is not to be the measure of our characters as soldiers." Provost guards had the duty of cleaning out disreputable places, insuring that soldiers had passes from their regiments, and "attend[ing] to moral publicans generally" (pp. 170, 180). Haines especially deplored dealing with drunk soldiers, presumably of the other regiments, and lamented that the men of the 44th had little time for amusements. "We are in a state of stagnation," he wrote. "We have not been so unhappy since the date of our enlistment as we have since we entered upon the police business at Newbern" (p. 171). However, as the time for their departure to Boston neared, Haines rejoiced that "we have had a hand in this glorious contest for the integrity of our country. No sacrifice or hardship we have endured balances the gratification of having done our country some service, however small or humble that service may have been." The "Corporal" advised the young men at home "to enlist voluntarily while a chance remains to identify yourselves in a glorious warfare" for the Union (p. 171).

Haines had an opportunity on provost-guard duty to observe closely local black society. New Bern, he told his readers, had become "the Mecca" for slaves escaping bondage. A census completed in March indicated that more that 8,500 blacks had sought refuge in New Bern and in three nearby camps. Haines reported that at night could be heard "the plaintive choral hymnings of devotional negroes in every direction, alone and in groups," and from open cabins, "the mingled voices of men wrestling painfully and agonizingly with the spirit" (p. 171). Haines was intrigued by the black custom of "waking" their dead. He wrote that mourners "sometimes render night so hideous by their songs and shoutings that the guard is attracted to the scene of their spiritual orgies, to enforce order" (p. 180).

The Corporal's illuminating experience with novitiate black troops in the Washington siege caused him to take a strong interest in the recruitment of the "African Brigade" at New Bern. Following President Lincoln's authorization in the Emancipation Proclamation for the enlistment of blacks, Colonel Lee wrote Colonel Robert Gould Shaw, commander of the 54th Massachusetts Volunteers, the first Northern black regiment to be organized, that "a brigade of coloured men could be easily raised in North Carolina." Colonel Lee also wrote Governor Andrew, who had asked about officers for the 54th, that his regiment was "a mine of military wealth to the State" and could be drawn upon for officers in black units.[58] Encouraged by this information, Governor Andrew, who had long advocated the recruitment of free blacks in the North, proposed that "some able, brave, tried, and believing man" be sent to North Carolina to recruit black troops. In April, the War Department authorized Colonel, later General, Edward A. Wild to raise a brigade of blacks in North Carolina.[59] With his headquarters at New Bern, Wild in May began to recruit three regiments of eastern North Carolina blacks, many of whom were slave refugees in New Bern, Washington, Plymouth, and other Federal-occupied river towns. The ranks of the 1st North Carolina Colored Volunteers filled rapidly. Wild, however, had to recruit in eastern Virginia in order to raise some of the troops for the 2nd and 3rd NCCV regiments. Even before the recruitment had been completed, the 55th Massachusetts Colored Regiment joined the three North Carolina regiments to form the African Brigade. During the summer Wild's brigade participated in the unsuccessful Federal campaign against Charleston and later, in an independent action, raided a guerrilla stronghold in northeastern North Carolina, freeing 2,500 slaves, seizing arms and provisions, and burning four rebel camps.[60]

For Haines, the "recruiting fever [that] has seized the freedmen of New Bern" provided a marvelous illustration of the new national commitment to freedom in the Civil War. He rejoiced that "the noble inspiration of human liberty is with us in this war. It helps us to abide temporary disaster, and is our pledge of final success." But, he warned, "we shall find a path stony and blood-moistened [if] we fail to have mercy and deal justly with the unoffending [black] people who are the innocent cause of this war" (p. 174). Though he did not volunteer to serve in a black regiment, Haines expressed pleasure that one officer and several enlisted men in his regiment had joined the African Brigade as junior officers.

June 6, 1863, the happy day of departure for home, finally came for the nine-month troops of the 44th Massachusetts. General Foster tried to persuade "the boys" to reenlist at New Bern in a new artillery regiment, but most of them wanted to go home before considering reenrollment in the army. Though he was disappointed in the 44th's response, Foster, along with his staff, turned out at the New Bern depot to praise the men for their service in his army and to wish them well.

After "as pleasant a sail as could be desired by anyone," unlike the voyage to North Carolina in 1862, the 44th regiment arrived home on June 9.[61] Of the 1,018 men in the regiment who went south in October, 902 returned to the Bay State, a high rate that reflected the regiment's social and educational status, its esprit de corps, and the competent leadership of its officers, particularly Colonel Lee. The fact that the term of service was only nine months also contributed to the impressive retention rate. Eight men died of battle wounds and twenty-four succumbed to diseases, including the regiment's surgeon, Robert Ware, scion of a prominent Boston family. None had become prisoners of war. Eighty-one had been discharged for various reasons, and three had deserted.[62] These losses also represented a rather low rate for a Federal unit in the war, and it was slightly below average for the seventeen nine-month regiments from Massachusetts serving in 1862–63.[63]

The 44th Massachusetts returned triumphantly to Boston. Reversing the order of their march in leaving the city more than seven months earlier, the troops, with a local militia escort and a band, paraded down streets crowded with men and women who cheered and showered them with flowers.[64] Assembling at the Boston Common, Mayor Frederic W. Lincoln welcomed the 44th home. He declared that their brave and stalwart service in North Carolina had defied the critics who claimed that "the habits and associations of a metropolitan life" unfitted city boys "for those stern duties and personal physical labors which they must endure in a soldier's career." After remarks by Colonel Lee thanking the city for the marvelous homecoming reception, the troops stacked their arms and, while greeting their families and friends, consumed the food and refreshments spread before them by Boston women. They were granted brief furloughs and ordered to report to Readville for mustering out of the Federal army on June 18. Corporal Haines's account of the 44th ended with the mustering out.

The 44th regiment's service in the state militia, however, continued until the end of the war. Indeed, a month after its return from the South, in mid-July, Governor Andrew called out the 44th regiment, along with other militia units, to prevent violence in Boston and nearby towns at the time of the New York Draft Riot. Upon the governor's request, Federal troops in nearby garrisons were brought into Boston. Colonel Lee assembled the 44th regiment at its Boylston Hall armory and awaited orders. As in New York, the enforcement in July of the Federal conscription law, combined with Lincoln's emancipation policy, inflamed thousands of men and women in the North, particularly Irish Democrats in the eastern cities who were opposed to the war and hostile to blacks. In Boston, an angry mob, reportedly between 4,000 and 5,000, including women, stormed the armory on Cooper Street, where a unit of Federal troops awaited them inside the building. The troops fired into the crowd, killing eight and wounding many others. This brief military action restored the peace in Boston, though scattered violence occurred elsewhere in the city.[65] Colonel Lee sent out pickets and "reconnoitering parties" from Boylston Hall, but the 44th regiment played no direct role in suppressing the violence.[66]

One hundred and seventy-three of the men of the 44th Massachusetts rejoined the Federal army. Sixty-eight of them served as officers in their units, an unusually large number but not surprising in view of the relatively high educational and social level of the men in the regiment. Thirty-one former members of the 44th became casualties, including nine who were killed in action and three who died in prisoner-of-war camps. Nineteen members of Haines's Company D reenlisted; Haines was not one of them.[67] Upon his discharge from the 44th, the "Corporal" returned to his position at the *Boston Herald*. After the war he moved back to Maine, where in 1879 he was the editor of a newspaper in Phillips. Crippled for the last nineteen years of his life, Haines moved about in a wheelchair. He never married. During the 1870s he applied for a military pension, but no record that he received one has been found. Haines evidently did not participate in the annual reunions of the 44th, which began in 1876 on the anniversary of the battle of Kinston. He died on September 29, 1900.[68]

The account of the 44th Massachusetts that Haines wrote and sent to the *Boston Herald* has provided us with a marvelous firsthand record of a unique and interesting nine-month Union regiment in America's greatest war. It offers an important description of the transformation of young, middle-class urban men into citizen soldiers willing and able to fight for the Union cause. With strong support from home and with respected local men as officers, the 44th, as much as any unit in the Federal army, represented a community gone to war. In training near their homes, the men of the 44th quickly subordinated their individualism to the common good and developed a strong unit cohesion. When they encountered a grim physical environment and hard combat in North Carolina, they lost their romantic notions about the war but not their devotion to the Union cause. Lincoln's emancipation policy, announced soon after the regiment's arrival in the South, reinforced the men's commitment to the defense of the republic. Indeed, despite the fact that many of them held racial prejudices, they became strong advocates of emancipation and the recruitment of blacks in the Federal army. Several members of the regiment later served and died in General Edward A. Wild's African Brigade.

This commitment to Union and freedom, embedded in their New England republican and religious tradition and combined with the rapid development of unit cohesion in camp, strengthened the resolve of the men of the 44th when faced with the rigors of marching through the difficult North Carolina lowlands and engaging the enemy in combat. Perhaps General Foster did not exaggerate when he declared that the 44th regiment performed more courageously and ably in battle than any other nine-month unit in North Carolina. Though the War Department remained skeptical of the desirability of nine-month troops, the effective service of the 44th Massachusetts Volunteer Militia Regiment demonstrated its value to the Federal cause during late 1862 and early 1863 when the tide of war seemingly had turned against the Union and long-term enlistments in the army had appreciably declined. The 44th Massachusetts, along with other nine-month regiments from the Northeast, aided in defeating the Confederate effort to drive Federal forces from eastern North Carolina during this critical period, thereby protecting the flank of the major Union army in Virginia and preserving important coastal bases for the Federal blockading fleet. Less than a month after the 44th Massachusetts Regiment disbanded, the war in the East turned against the South—at Gettysburg.

CHAPTER 1

At Readville, Massachusetts

In Barracks at Readville,

SATURDAY, AUG. 30, 1862.

Your readers in Boston will not be uninterested in following the fortunes of the gallant 44th, which has just gone forth from your city with full ranks, made up in large measure of young men in whose honor and welfare every true Bostonian will feel a peculiar interest. The *personnel* of the 44th (recruited up from the Fourth Battalion of Infantry as a nucleus,) has been so frequently the subject of newspaper remark, that nothing more need be said under that head; but it may not be vainglorious to say that no regiment has gone forth from the old Bay State, renowned for the quality of its soldiers, which exceeds or equals the second New England Guard regiment, as regards the personal qualities of its rank and file. All the learned professions are represented in its ranks, and even some of the recondite sciences and fine arts have their accomplished devotees in this corps. Among the latter may be reckoned the astronomer [Horace P.]

Tuttle, of Cambridge, and the brothers [Cyrus and Darius] Cobb, artists, of Boston. We have sons of ministers and millionaires, and many rich men in their own rights. The sons of ministers in the 44th, grievous to say, are generally publicans themselves, and give few signs of eminently Christian training. This is strange.

> *"Tis true, 'tis pity:*
> *And pity tis, tis true."*

This is the second attempt which the Fourth Battalion has recently made to do their country some service; and we have been wondering if the present will prove as futile as the preceding one. But these do not cover the honorable record of the Fourth Bats. The Massachusetts 24th sprang from this Battalion. That and the 2nd and other Massachusetts regiments of earlier and later dates have been largely officered from its ranks. It has provided the army of the Union *two hundred and twenty-five commissioned officers.* A fact more extraordinary in connection with one military organization cannot be adduced, and will go far to render the Fourth historic. The youthful patriot, [S. W.] Putnam, whose untimely sacrifice at Ball's Bluff, considered in connection with the unusual sweetness and force of character of the young martyr, has caused the tears of a nation to flow, was once a member of the Fourth, and his portrait now graces the walls of its armory.[1]

The 44th came one day too soon to barrack at Readville, but it was their own fault. The fine new barracks just erected there were not completed, and will not be until to-night, although now habitable and comfortable as heart can desire. But we have all had to work to produce this comfortable state of affairs so early, and the "school of the soldier" has been neglected today.

Our first night in barracks was exceedingly jolly, as was to have been expected. Poor devils who depend on good sleep and a good deal of it for what vitality they can muster, might probably have sworn last night, if they had been obliged to barrack at Readville. Not that the boys were riotous, or even obstreperous, but simply jolly. We supped on hard bread, and coffee hotter than the crater of Vesuvius. Then, pipes and cigars

Unidentified company of the 44th Massachusetts Regiment, the day before the regiment was mustered out of the Federal army. Courtesy of the United States Army Military History Institute, Carlisle Barracks, Pennsylvania

lighted, the early evening was devoted to music—songs of home. After we had retired to our bunks, music of another character "beguiled" the hours of night.

Your correspondent slept not at all the first night in barrack, for obvious reasons. The inside musical performances opened with a barn-yard chorus by the entire company, followed by a rapid, unintermitting succession of dog, hog, pig, and rooster solos, duetts and quartettes, single and combined, which continued in great volume until the unexpected arrival of the captain and his lieutenants, who are unfortunately without any ear for music. After a short intermission, the performance was resumed in a greatly modified condition, commencing with admirable imitations of chickens astray from the shelter of the maternal wing, and coming to a pause with the low, small, satisfied twitterings of chickens in clover.

Then followed sounds less artistic, but not less suggestive to the general appreciation, intermingled with snatches of conversation of a highly festive character. The good wit of the occasion rendered endurable what would otherwise have been an intolerable nuisance to any one wanting sleep so badly as your humble servant; but at last, as it must be confessed, even this element failed to satisfy a scientific audience. Objurgations, not loud but deep, came from a number of bunks where sleep had failed to come, or tarried a moment to be cruelly banished. Despite all these adverse circumstances, sound sleep actually came to one poor fellow sleeping unsuspectingly below the "Corporal;" but, as the Fates would have it, it departed from him in this wise.

A small britannia flask, used chiefly to contain coffee and milk in the temporary absence of dippers, fell from the rear of the "Corporal's" bunk directly upon the head of the sleeper, suddenly arousing him to the consciousness of life and its uncertainties. He screamed out vigorously that one of the slats of our bunk had fallen upon his head, and sarcastically offered to get up a contribution to improve our sleeping accommodations, and thereby render his own safety more complete. The "Corporal," who felt the flask slip from beneath his pillow, knew that the aroused man labored under a misapprehension, and clambered down to recover the fugitive vessel, and manipulate a suddenly prominent bump on the cranium of the one man of company D who succeeded in getting asleep.

To-day we have been applying finishing touches to our quarters, and exercising in company movements, by squads, &c. The turn-out at beat of *reveille,* this morning at five o'clock, was a new sensation even to the "Corporal." The style of the morning ablutions was a novelty, too. Instead of basins and soap at the barracks, we were ordered to "fall in with towels," and then were positively marched to a pond to wash our faces and hands! O, the degradation of military rule! Such is war.

To-morrow we shall look for a host of friends from Boston. We will not attempt to disguise the hope we cherish, that they may bring their pockets full of apples!

In the multiplicity of Colonels Lee, never *lees* in a military sense, your correspondent may inform somebody by stating that the Colonel Lee commanding the 44th, was Major [Francis L.] Lee of the 4th Battalion, and never Colonel Lee of the 20th or 27th, or Colonel [Henry] Lee of the Governor's

Colonel Francis L. Lee. Courtesy of the United States Army Military
History Institute, Carlisle Barracks, Pennsylvania.

Staff, but is a brother of the latter. He is a large-hearted man, and a splendid officer. His staff and line officers are fully worthy of him. Altogether we are eminently satisfied with ourselves as a regiment.

In Barracks at Readville,

SEPT. 6, 1862.

Our first Sunday in barracks was enlivened by the presence of friends from Boston. The hope we breathed with respect to apples was more than met. The last cigar in many a private stock had just ended in smoke, and shed its sweetness on the desert air of Readville, haply to be succeeded by new relays at the hands of thoughtful friends. Wine, fruit and other comestibles poured into some favored messes with overwhelming abundance, and it must be confessed that Monday's bill of health was not improved by Sunday's too luxurious bill of fare. "Corporal" would suggest that pastry and cake are of no benefit to a soldier, but that ripe fruit is not only a luxury, but of great advantage as a corrective of the system.

Another sanitary suggestion. Several sick men on Monday traced their ill health to bathing too soon after dinner. Few men can safely plunge into the water within four hours after eating heartily. It stops the digestive machinery, and then all goes wrong, indefinitely. Just before dinner is a good time to bathe, or just before breakfast or supper will do.

Would any one like to know how our first dress parade went off? Well, I shan't tell. The occasion was graced by the Boston Brass Band; but a spirited young horse in front of the lines did the best thing of the day—dancing in perfect time to the music. With his head erect and nervously distended nostrils, he was a picture of grace. That that horse has a soul "Corporal" has no doubt, else how could he have music in it? Horses of duller metal were all around him, standing upon three legs, and doing nothing but switch their tails at the flies. Some human beings behave still more indifferently at concerts.

There is some emulation among the companies in the way of neatness, conveniences and decorations about their several barracks. The palm is due to Company D for an early display of flags upon the outside, and also for certain novel decorations of the interior in the shape of one or two delicate articles of apparel, probably wafted by the wind from a washing hung out to dry.

One of our fellows was attacked by a cow the other day, and badly wounded in his under-garments, but is expected to recover.

Company D has paid a little compliment to its commissioned officers. Captain [Henry D.] Sullivan was made the recipient of a sword, sash, and belt, and to Lieutenants [James H.] Blake and [Asa H.] Stebbins were presented shoulder straps.[2] These gentlemen are justly beloved by the men of their company for their entire devotion to duty, and their high accomplishments as officers. They are all graduates of the Fourth Battalion. Of the qualifications of Captains [Charles] Hunt, [Jacob H.] Lombard and [Joseph R.] Kendall also, the personal acquaintance of your correspondent enables him to speak in terms of high praise.[3]

Company F having had the temerity to erect a flag-staff taller than Company D's, the latter company extended its mast a few feet over that of its neighboring barrack. This ambition to excel exhibits itself in a variety of ways. Some of the barracks are prettily lighted with lanterns, and in one or two of them the bunks are lettered and ornamented in a very artistic manner. Afterward Captain Spencer Richardson's boys secured the tallest pole which could be found in the neighboring woods, and at the present writing their flag floats the highest. The barracks occupied by the companies of Captain Lombard, Captain Hunt and Captain Kendall also have creditable displays of bunting, and contribute to give the encampment an animated and beautiful appearance.

Each company has its excellent choir of singers, but Company F affords instrumental as well as vocal music. The Cobb brothers, who are excellent violinists, nightly delight a numerous auditory assembled about their bunks.

As our stay at Readville protracts, we are gathering about us many little comforts and luxuries which we shall probably have to sacrifice in the event of a sudden retirement from before an enemy. But while we stay here our purpose is to make ourselves extremely comfortable; and in this purpose a numerous constituency of friends are lending their assistance in the way of hampers and baskets and bundles of fruit, and other delicacies. *Our* mess gratefully acknowledges a basket of incomparable pies from a pious lady in Boston, who has no peer among modern pastry cooks. Our judgment condemns all such luxuries, but our heart acknowledges how good they are. And we are most generously remembered in gifts of more substantial value—writing desks, medicines, wax-tapers, smoking caps, pipes, tobacco, cigars, &c., &c. All these, we know, are the romance of war, the pleasant prelude of things considerably rougher, but we will enjoy them while we may, and when we come to the sterner duties of the soldier our hearts and arms shall be nerved to strength by all the thoughtful kindness which friends now lavish upon us.

We shall not forget the "Donation Committee" of the city of Boston, or its queenly agent who presides at the headquarters on Tremont street, and dispenses havelocks, Testaments, pins, needles, towels, handkerchiefs, &c., to every applicant whom it is in her power to serve.[4]

I informed you in my first letter that our regiment was honored by the membership of the astronomer Tuttle; I omitted, however, to mention that he rejected the tender of a lucrative position in the Washington Observatory to do a private soldier's duty in the 44th Regiment. Patriotism more self-sacrificing than this is rarely to be found, but when found, a note should be made of it at once. We propose to call our astronomical comrade "Old Stars." Although not yet twenty-three years old, he has already grown gray in his assiduous night-watches for the starry voyagers of the upper deep; and now his chief anxiety is to be placed upon the round of the night sentinel, where he may pursue his favorite study.

We have been having some delicious days this week. It was pleasure enough to live in such atmosphere and sunlight. Our evenings, too, have been delightful, and we have had with them the music of the band, promenades, dancing, &c. Many friends, with beautiful turnouts, and without, have visited us, and we have had a wonderfully happy week. Who shall describe the wonderful beauty of these September sunrises, and the exhilaration of the morning air and bath at the pond?

On Thursday we were honored by a visit from a sub-committee of the Citizens' Committee of Boston, deputed to investigate the cuisine of this regiment. Reports had gone abroad that we were badly fed: that, in point of fact, we were not allowed broiled chickens for breakfast, nor roast beef and plum-pudding for dinner. It is barely possible that the committee had even more serious charges to investigate, and were horrified to discover that we had neither loaf-sugar or cream in our tea and coffee. Notwithstanding these serious deficiencies, the committee were constrained to confess that our bread and soup were good enough for the guests of the Parker House, and that in all other respects we fared as well as the soldiers of any other regiment. We certainly didn't know that we were badly used, until we were honored by the visit of the gentlemen of eminent gravity. We *would* whisper one word in the ear of the cook, and ask him to cook the rice; but for the consolation of that amiable individual we would remind him of the remark of Thomas Jefferson, that there was but one woman north of the Potomac who knew how to perform this important culinary operation.

The time of our departure, as well as our destination, is still problematical. Some have it that we are going to Virginia, others to Baltimore, others to New Orleans, and others that we are to remain where we are for a considerable space of time. The work of drill has commenced in earnest, and in a few weeks, few regiments will excel the 44th in thoroughness of instruction. We have received our guns (Enfield rifles), although they have not yet been distributed. A portion of our uniforms have arrived, and will soon be distributed. A large number of the regiment will wear uniforms made to measure, and of better stock than that furnished by Uncle Sam.

Before we leave Readville, it is suggested that we give our friends a grand parting reception and ball, and that an acre or two of the campground be floored over for the convenience of those who would like to trip the light fantastic.[5]

In Barracks at Readville,

SEPT. 13, 1862.

It may interest your readers to know that the field occupied by the 44th Regiment is where the famous striped pig was exhibited twenty odd years ago—the pig made immortal in the well remembered song commencing—

In Dedham just now there was a great muster,
Which gathered the people all up in a cluster;
A terrible time, and what do you think,
To find a way to get something to drink!
Ri tu, di nu, di nu, &c.

To-day traffickers in the ardent hereabout labor under similar embarrassments with those of 1840. Colonel Lee has military jurisdiction over a territorial radius of one mile, and has no bowels of compassion for those fellows who open rum and refreshment booths along the highways and in the bushes about the camp. "Corporal" has already signalized himself by leading a squad of men and assisting in the confiscation and reduction of a liquor shanty romantically situated among the pines in the vicinity. The operation yielded us one flask of whisky, two empty flasks, and a fresh supply of needed lumber, whereof "Corporal" was awarded one board in consideration of his gallantry on the occasion alluded to.

Another new sensation has befallen your correspondent in his first experience as corporal of the guard. We have had a succession of magnificent days and nights since we went into camp, and guard duty has not been the most disagreeable part of our experience as soldiers. The calm majesty of these moon-lit nights, the brooding stillness occasionally broken by the challenge of the sentinel in this and the neighboring camps, and the white tents and garrisons dotting the dark field, conspire to form a scene of impressive beauty.

We have received an order from the Commander-in-Chief of all the forces in Massachusetts prohibiting us from bathing at all Christian hours of the day, out of regard to the sensitive nerves of somebody.[6] As nobody but soldiers live near the ponds, it is to be supposed that the order was promulgated as a measure of consideration of the naiads and nymphs habitant hereabout. We heartily wish that everybody was like Caesar's wife.[7]

The "women of America," including a few Boston friends, have sent us in a grand lunch of Washington pies [a layer cake with cream or jam filling], coffee and cold meats. Where these dainties went to is a profound mystery to the non coms. and privates, but it is doubtless "all right."

At dress parade, the other day, Miss Josie Gregg, of Boston, through Colonel Lee, presented us an elegant flag, and the gift was acknowledged by three cheers. Captain Spencer Richardson has received a sword, sash, &c., from friends of the Mercantile Library Association, of which he is an ex-president. Orderly [Horace S.] Stebbins, of Company F, brother of Lieutenant Stebbins, of Company D, has received a sword, sash, &c., from members of his company. Dan. Simpson, the drummer, has received from friends in Company C (Captain Lombard), a Turkish fez, which gives old Dan. a very rakish appearance.

Flag competition continues, and now every barrack shows its bunting—that of Company D again floating the highest. Thursday morning Company F's flag-staff presented to the eyes of an astonished camp the same small white, bifurcated garment which had previously served to decorate the interior of a neighboring barrack. The boys are bound not to "have their selves," as Uncle Sim Wilbur used to say. We now hope, however, for better things for our company, having sent the sergeants to a tent by themselves, and conferred the responsibility of keeping good order upon the corporals.

Captain James Richardson's company give their barrack a beautiful, almost oriental appearance at evening, by the introduction of numerous Chinese lanterns.[8] In every barrack the fine arts are still cultivated in the lettering and ornamentation of the bunks. One is labelled "Squirrels' Nest;" another, "Penguin's Nest;" another, "Sleeping Beauties;" another, "Siamese Twins;" another, "Damon and Pythias." Some graduates of Tufts College, who occupy a bunk together, inform the world in good classical phrase that it is sweet to die for your country. They may well say that, if living in the barracks at Readville be dying for your country. "Corporal" cannot but look with amazement upon these classical young patriots elevated upon their bunks and devouring home danties [dainties] over this conspicuous motto—"*Dulce et decorum est pro patrioe mori!*" [With sweetness and grace, it is to die for one's country].

In Company D we have the following graduates and under-graduates of Tufts College:—E. Fitz Gerald, Portsmouth, New Hampshire; C. Adams, Middleton, North Carolina;[9] J. B. Brewster, Plymouth; W. E. Savery, South Carver; W. C. Ireland, Boston; W. E. Gibbs, West Cambridge, Massachusetts; W. P. Treat, Canton, Maine; and A. C. Fish, Janesville, Wisconsin. As may be supposed they are ornaments to the company and regiment. Mr. Gibbs relinquishes the pastorate of the Universalist Church in West Cambridge and a liberal salary to serve his country as a private soldier.

Our Chaplain, Rev. Mr. [Edward H.] Hall, of Plymouth, was introduced to us last Sunday, and made a good impression upon the regiment for his brevity of speech and avoidance of religious cant. He said the engrossing duty of the day was devotion to our country, and felicitated the young men of the regiment that an opportunity was opened to them to consecrate their powers to so high an object. The music was very humdrum, considering the number and quality of our vocalists, but we shall do better.

Mr. Charles White, of Milton, who has two sons in the 44th, is getting up a regimental song book. Original contributions of the true ring would doubtless be well received.

The quarters of Company G, Captain Hunt, are tastefully ornamented with evergreen, and are much admired by visitors; but it is on [?] all hands conceded that the barrack of Company D, thanks to the oversight of our admirable Corporal [Rodolph C.] Waterman, is most noticeable for its complete order and neatness. It is whispered that we are to have a piano, if we remain here much longer; and then, with such singers among us as

Charley Ewer, from the Warren Street [Boston] choir, we reckon upon very good times in the musical line.

Yesterday was a great day with the men of the 44th. We were mustered into the service of the United States by companies. The event was hailed with cheering and general rejoicing; and then the uniforms provided by Uncle Sam were opened for inspection. Many members of the regiment had already provided themselves with garments of superior quality, made to measure, and those who had not taken this precaution regretted it the more when they came to see the half cotton, shoddy, slouchy stuff sent to them through the State authorities. Colonel Lee, who has a natural abhorrence of shams in all shapes, advised his men not to draw such uniforms, and promised to assist them in procuring garments made to measure. The men gladly acted upon the suggestion of the Colonel and will clothe themselves, not less as a matter of neatness and taste than of economy.

The mustering-in certificates were given out yesterday and to-day, and some of the boys have already pocketed the generous bounties voted them in Boston and elsewhere. Mayor [Joseph M.] Wightman was here on Friday, and was cheered as he passed among the barracks.

Last evening the barrack of Company F, Captain [Charles] Storrow, was the centre of attraction. The parents of the artists Cobb were present, and the delighted spectators of a country break-down and other festive demonstrations. Mrs. Cobb delivered a little impromptu poem, and Mr. Cobb a very stirring address, both of which were vociferously applauded. The Cobb brothers sang and played exquisitely, and the occasion was one of touching interest.

Brigadier-General [R. A.] Pierce [Peirce] has been appointed to command Camp Meigs, including the several encampments at Readville, and Lieutenant Richard H. Weld, Post Adjutant.

To-day a fine flag-staff was erected at the brigade headquarters near the depot. In a little while Camp Meigs will be one of the grandest and most complete military posts in New England.

We have been provided with muskets for guard duty only, and of course have much work to perform in the manual of arms' drill before we shall be fit to take the field. In the facings, we have made commendable progress, and have been highly complimented by Colonel Lee in this respect.[10]

Since the 44th went into barracks they have been favored with the services of the Boston Brass Band, under the lead of Mr. Flagg. It is said the expense is to be defrayed by an assessment upon the regiment. Considering that the mass of the regiment have had no voice in the selection of a band, a number of persons are inclined to consider this a little "rough." What "Corporal" and many others wish to suggest in this connection is, that a few of our rich friends in Boston unite to defray the expense of a *good* band, which shall accompany us to the seat of war. It is thought they would be pleased to confer this substantial benefit upon the regiment, and thus acknowledge the important assistance rendered by the Fourth Battalion of Infantry in raising the quota of Boston. Failing in this, a set of instruments would be gratefully acknowledged, and an excellent band would then be recruited from the regiment.

In Barracks at Readville,

SATURDAY, SEPT. 20, 1862.

We begin to feel the rigors of a soldier's life, and among our hardships are green corn, onion soup, baked beans, brown bread, boiled potatoes, &c. If we had not been mustered in at the time we were, there is no saying what the consequences of delay might not have been. As for our cook, he has been forced to seek an asylum out of camp, under a pretence of sickness. He could no longer face the frown of a virtuous and half-starved soldiery, so he unwreathed his face of "that smile," which had so long deceived the boys, and then—

Folded up his dishcloth like the Arabs,
And in darkness stole away.

Applications for the vacancy at the "Bite Tavern," from Parker & Mills and J. B. Smith are under consideration.

Since we were sworn in we have felt the tightening of the military rein. No man has been allowed to see his friends, or to receive presents from them except on the points of their bayonets. On Monday about two hundred men only could be mustered for battalion drill. The other eight hundred, except those who had gone to Boston and elsewhere, were in irons at the guard-house. Colonel Lee and staff were intoxicated—with the varied strains of the Boston Brass Band. Altogether we have been in a sad muss.

When are we going to leave for the seat of war? We don't know. It is said at the [state] Adjutant-General's office that we shall be the next regiment to leave. If this is so, why are not the muskets given out? The Elementary Spelling Book used to say, "wheels are admirable instruments of conveyance." It might also have said that guns are useful implements of warfare, and that wheelings and facings alone never did kill the devil. "Corporal," who confesses to a distaste for actual warfare, and who, like Sparrowgrass, would be glad never to leave his State, except in case of invasion, indulges the hope that this delay in distributing the arms indicates an indefinite continuance of barrack life and drill.[11]

The past week has been one of furloughs, the men being thus enabled to go to their several hailing places and procure their bounties. We are sorry to say that red tape has ruled potently with some of the town authorities, and that some soldiers have been disappointed in not receiving what is clearly theirs, for the want of forms of certificate not required in Boston. Dear old Boston! She not only does generous things, but does them as quietly and with as little trouble to the recipients as though she was not conferring a benefit. She that never tires in doing good is not misnamed "the Hub." "Corporal" will be her spokesman, although his bounty came not from her treasury, nor any other as yet.

We reasonably expect that a week of furloughs will be succeeded by work. Some of our little captains are threatening us hard. More drill and less guard duty will not be unacceptable to the poor fellows, whose duty as sentinels for the past week has only been relieved by the relaxation of police guard work or scavenger service. Bootless has been the plea, "I was on guard yesterday, and police guard the day before." The orderly knew it. There was no help for it. It costs hard work, but we have the cleanest camp in Christendom, if we may believe visitors. Lieutenant [N. B.] McLaughlin, our mustering-in officer, was profuse in his commendations of the 44th. It was, he said, the most orderly and the cleanest regiment he ever mustered in. The company rolls were the neatest which had ever come under his inspection, and the number of absentees (one sick and one unavoidably absent) the smallest in his experience. We do not wish to be always elevating our horn, but we must record history.

Speaking of guard duty, we have added to our guards another wheel in the camp machinery of good order—a provost guard. Captain [John A.] Smith, of Company H, has been appointed Provost Marshal of this post. Lieutenant [Frank H.] Forbes, of Company K, formerly of the Commercial Bulletin, Lieutenant Laughton, of the 43d Regiment, and Lieutenant Singleton, of the 42d, have been appointed Lieutenants of the provost guard. The headquarters of this guard are near the depot. It consists of a relief from each of the above regiments, and its principal duty is to reduce rum booths in the vicinity and look up stragglers from the camp.

Since my last letter there have been added to the list of decorated barracks those of Company B, Captain [John M.] Griswold, and Company A, Captain [Spencer] Richardson. Company D has introduced Chinese lanterns, small flags, and the arms of the New England Guards, neatly painted by one of our numerous artists, to wit, Fred. Sayer, the lingual prodigy and pet of his corps. We have not yet procured a drummer, but our tallest corporal, [Elmer A.] Messinger, who has seen enough of military preferment, is in training as a candidate. Since the above was written, a drummer has been selected, but Messinger's claims were ignored.

Among the testimonials of the past week have been a sword, sash and belt to Orderly [Frank W.] Hatch, of Captain Hunt's company, and a splendid meerschaum pipe to Captain James Richardson. Gold, silver and amber combine to make the latter present a dudheen [duheen] of irreproachable beauty.[12]

A startling rumor has just come into camp to the effect that we are to be allowed no more extras. The fellows who have been subsisting upon pies, sponge cake, pickles, etc., etc., propose to hold an indignation meeting, and arouse public sentiment against the contemplated outrage. If we cannot be allowed to eat *Washington* pies, what are our liberties worth, we should like to know? More than this, we are not to be allowed to eat our rations in barrack except in rainy weather. Such is war. But are we to be kept under stricter discipline than regiments in the field? Are we to have no sutler? Is the dealer in "vegetable oysters" opposite the guard house to be driven off?[13] We refuse to believe it.

A large proportion of the regiment is now uniformed in neatly fitting suits, having no relationship to the contractors' shoddy which was attempted to be foisted upon us. Our appearance at the dress parades is creditable, and every pleasant afternoon crowds of spectators honor us with their presence. The number of pretty girls that adorn these occasions, coming as they do, laden with offerings of fruits and flowers for their favorites, is by no means the least interesting feature of the afternoon displays. The angels even besiege us in our barracks, and although we are delighted to see them, they seem sometimes to forget that we have no retiring rooms, and that we must perforce make our toilettes in our bunks, or not make them at all. "Corporal" wants it distinctly understood that he don't care anything about this, personally. He speaks for the modest man of his company.

Yesterday the numerous flags at Camp Meigs were at half-mast in respect to the memory of General [Jesse L.] Reno.[14] To-day the Warren Drum Corps were rapturously received by the soldiers of the 44th. Doctor Kirk, the great and earnest-hearted minister of the Mount Vernon Church, was in camp to-day, distributing neat little books appropriate to soldiers. Neatly printed *books* are read when mere tracts are thrown away. "Corporal" heard one fellow remark with irreverent facetiousness that somebody had filled his booth with tracts and carried away all articles of extrinsic value. The chap had undoubtedly lost something, and selected this profane way of giving vent to his anger.

Your correspondent could expatiate by the half column of the social fascinations of this life in barracks, of the genial friendships formed; of the glorious hearts discovered; of the roaring wit brought out by this free and easy companionship; of the freedom from conventional restraints and the care of every-day pursuits. Do not, dear reader, think us too jolly and comfortable for soldiers, but rather thank Heaven for the sunny side and recompense of military life, which, perhaps, after all, but very feebly offset the shadows through which lies the pathway of him who takes up arms in defense of liberty, imperilled as it is to-day.

In Barracks at Readville,
SATURDAY, SEPT. 27, 1862.

One of our home corps was at Camp Meigs last Sunday, and noted the extraordinary rush of visitors upon that day. The members of the 44th were allowed a few hours' leave of absence outside their lines, and improved the time by visiting the encampments of the other regiments and battery east of the pond. The visit was an agreeable one, and afforded us a fine opportunity to contrast the condition of our camp with that of the other regiments at this post. We found the barracks of the 45th (Cadet Regiment) in fine condition, and constructed with better regard to light and ventilation than our own. In other respects we did not suffer by comparison with either regiment. Gilmore's Band honored us by playing the Fourth Battalion Quickstep. Gilmore promises us a serenade one of these fine evenings. In a few days more we shall have more moonlight nights, and, if we remain at Camp Meigs, a repetition of out-door evening sociability, music and moonlight rambles. At this writing, however, the air is thick with rumors of a speedy departure of our regiment. We have it from apparently good authority that the 47th, Colonel Marsh, is to occupy these barracks next week, and that a transport now lies in Boston harbor waiting to convey us to New Orleans, or Newbern, for one of which posts, it is said, we are to sail the latter part of next week. Another rumor sends us to Annapolis, preliminary to our sea voyage South, and another to Fort Warren. We propose to resign ourselves to either of these dispositions, especially to the New Orleans trip, now that we begin to feel the bite of these autumn nights and mornings. The most unmusical of sounds is the *reveille* at five o'clock, A.M. Even the freshness and magnificence of those star-gemmed mornings scarcely compensate us for this ghostly hour of turning out. But now we are threatened with calls among the small hours for the purpose of preparing us for surprises in the enemy's country. We would gladly excuse our officers from this laborious work in our behalf. In fact, we shall not be less grateful to them if they do not carry the plan into execution. Besides, midnight movements like these might excite the suspicion of our ubiquitous provost guard, and result in getting the whole regiment into limbo. We could not even visit our neighbors of the other regiments, last Sunday, without falling into the hands of those merciless Philistines, who go about the country like roaring lions seeking whom they may devour.

Companies E and D have been making double-quick marches to Dedham village by the three-mile route. An uninterrupted run of three miles is something incredible to the uninitiated. "Corporal" and five others confess, with proper self-abasement, that the last mile was rather too much for them, especially as your correspondent was tortured by a pair of new boots. We fell out. The first man who "caved in" was [Private Eli] Tucker—a coincidence worthy the notice of one of your cotemporaries [*sic*]. By seasonably falling out, we escaped rushes of blood, palpitations of the heart, and further abrasions of the feet, but we were soon placed in mortal terror of the provost guard. We saw their blue habiliments and burnished muskets in the distance, and rushed precipitately into the first wayside building. They did not discover us, but we saw their wagon enter the village of Dedham close upon the heels of those who had out-winded us. We fondly hoped that our comrades would get arrested—so amiable is human nature; but the guard saw their formidable numbers and passed by on the other side. In the place where Tucker and his fellow recusants sought seclusion, we were hospitably regaled with apples, and then soon after started upon our return to camp by another road. A tint of blue in the distance re-awakened our fears of the provost. We rushed into a barn and peeped through half-closed doors, until a lady in cerulean[15] garb drove past and relieved us of our immediate terror. A little further along, the familiar notification of "vegetable oysters and refreshments" induced us to invest in a bottle of pop beer. "Vegetable oysters," although loudly de-manded, were not to be had. At last the ill-disguised scorn of the woman who kept the place recommended us to leave. Who should we next en-counter but two soldiers? They doubtless belonged to the provost; but we put a bold face upon the matter, and determined to stand the chances. They were not the *provost.* They might think we were, so we demanded their passes in the most business-like manner we could assume, and they were produced, although not without manifest distrust of our functions. We pronounced the passes satisfactory, and then proceeded camp-ward with aching sides and manifestations of severe colic, which further excited the suspicions of the two artillerymen with passes. A little while before dinner, a small "awkward squad" might have been seen descending the railroad embankment near Camp Meigs, and then proceeding, crab-like, by the right and left flanks, until it safely passed the lines. The main party had not arrived, and we confidently reported them in the hands of the provost. On the contrary, as we learned upon their arrival, they had been detained by a number of beautiful Samaritans habitant along the road, who came out laden with apples and pears, which were distributed among the soldiers with smiles and kind words. Several fellows came back to camp with hearts and pedal extremities equally damaged.

Our rifles have been distributed at last, and we have commenced drill-ing in the manual with great industry. We are going strictly by "the book," and have to unlearn some things peculiar to the tactics of Colonel [Tho-mas G.] Stevenson, formerly of the Fourth Battalion. This gentleman, by the way, visited us on Wednesday, and was cordially received. If he had arrived at the time he was expected, a formal demonstration by the entire regiment would have been made in his honor. We were all drawn up in line for that purpose, but it is not improbable that "Tom," as his old military *confreres* fondly call him, got wind of the proceeding.

The rumors given in my last concerning stricter camp discipline were chiefly true. We are not allowed to eat in the barracks. The order concerning extras from home has not been rigidly enforced, and our friends have been allowed to remember us with many little comforts, and to assist at many delightful messes in the company streets. As a screw has lately worked loose in the matter of rations, it must be confessed that these attentions from our friends have proved most fortunate. Some of the boys will have it that the interests of the regimental sutler were consulted in the late promulgation about provisions in the barracks, and several companies have voted not to patronize that individual. It is certainly difficult to conceive why dainties from home are more objectionable in a military point of view than those from the sutler's stores. In this connection, "Corporal" would state that Company D, in the matter of rations, owes much to the liberality of Corporal [Thaddeus] Page.

On Thursday we had a grand cleaning out of barracks. Everything was removed from them, and exposed to the air and sunshine. Most of the regiment being absent on escort duty, the task devolved upon a few. It was a work of vandalism. Cherished shelves, pictures, flags, and flowers came down at one fell swoop. The personal effects of absentees were tumbled down and bestowed in promiscuous piles into the bunks, and then carried outside. They comprised a heterogeneous collection of valuables, like pats of butter, soap, packs of cards and Testaments, tooth-brushes and cutlery, spare clothing and baskets, haversacks, havelocks, night-caps and smoking-caps, pipes, tobacco and matches, now and then a bottle, and one umbrella. Having the example before them of the army in Flanders, the absentees of the 44th swore [cursed] when they came back and witnessed the "improvements" which had been made while they were away.

We have occasional evening entertainments here in the shape of ground and lofty tumbling (*en costume*) and sparring matches. Between our hours of drill, camp duties, reception of visitors, music, letter-writing, &c., there is no possibility of time dragging upon our hands. Now visitors are restricted to the hours between half past four and half past eight P.M. Among the testimonials of the past week was the presentation to Orderly [George L.] Tripp, of Company D (Captain Sullivan) of a beautiful sword, sash and belt. The company are much attached to their orderly for his modest and efficient way of performing the many and arduous duties appertaining to his post. Orderly [Clarence] Sumner, of Captain [Joseph R.] Kendall's company, who is also highly spoken of, has received a similar compliment.

Our Surgeon, Dr. [Robert] Ware, of Boston, is drawing a tight rein over the regiment. His experience upon the Peninsula has given him notions of sanitary discipline which some think too severe for soldiers in barracks at home. He has stripped our quarters of everything but prime necessaries, and we are reduced to a very bald condition indeed. We shall probably see the wisdom of this severity more clearly by and by. At present a majority of the boys don't see it at all. Thursday night we tried the experiment of sleeping without straw in our bunks. It didn't work, and now we propose to provide ourselves with canvas bags to keep the straw in place, and thus avoid the continual nuisance of straw litter inside and out.

On Thursday detachments from six companies of our regiment acted as escort at the funeral of the late Lieutenant-Colonel [Wilder] Dwight.[16] Considering the short time of our practice in the manual of arms, the regiment was awarded the credit of great proficiency, particularly in the firing of vollies. Colonel Stevenson paid the regiment the highest compliment.

Among other things for the convenience of the soldiers is the arrangement made by Brigadier-General Pierce [Peirce] to have two regular mails daily. Letters directed "Camp Meigs, Boston," with the letter of the company and the number of the regiment, will reach their destination promptly. Mails close in Boston at seven A.M., and two P.M. The arrangement thus far has worked admirably.

The Brigadier was serenaded last night by our band, which went to his quarters, accompanied by the Colonel, staff and line officers, all of whom received the hospitable courtesies of the commanding General.

On Friday the old members of the Fourth Battalion were pleased to witness the beaming countenance of ex-Adjutant [Charles C.] Soule, late military superintendent of plantations in South Carolina. Mr. Soule was Adjutant of the Battalion when it was sworn into the United States service last May. He now declares his intention of going with us as a private soldier. We shall be glad to welcome him into our ranks.[17]

In closing this letter, "Corporal" must acknowledge a kind and most substantial remembrancer from a noble woman in Clinton, whose gift was accompanied by a note full of sentiments of patriotism, and personal interest in the soldier. Her kindness will not be forgotten by your correspondent or his "mess."

In Barracks at Readville,

SATURDAY, OCT. 4, 1862.

The past week Col. Lee has wisely varied our drill by taking the regiment on marches through portions of the country surrounding Camp Meigs. Our first of these marches, after escort duty at the funeral of the late Lt. Col. Dwight, was through that portion of Milton of which we have such delightful glimpses from the camp. We were forced to breathe dust freely, but through the clouds which rose wherever the regiment moved we caught refreshing views of stately homesteads, blushing orchards, and autumn-tinted landscapes. We were halted a mile from camp, and treated to cool water in front of an elm-shaded farm house overlooking a bend in a smooth stream just where a herd of cows were enjoying their forenoon delectation. If they had arranged themselves for picturesque effect they couldn't have done better. If the reader would see apples upon the wayside trees "like apples of gold in pictures of silver," let him take a warm, dusty march of six miles past orchards laden with September fruitage. Since the march to Milton we have surprised the good people of Mill Village and round about Dedham Court House by a sudden appearance in their midst. For the gratification of our many friends who are anxiously watching the progress of this regiment, I have to report that our marching extorted great praise from Col. Lee, who, by the way, is quite as prompt to give us a sound blowing up as he is to compliment. In point of fact, he does neither by halves. His outspoken frankness and generosity are creating him hosts of warm friends in the regiment.

Our camp has not been without one or two episodes of "romance in real life," to coin a phrase. Last Sunday—a day exactly answering to the description of the poet—

"sad, and dark, and dreary,"

the camp of the 44th was visited by a pale fair one in quest of her "betrayer." Betrayer, a moustached young fellow not unknown among the Boston sports, attempted to play the stranger. The dodge was unsuccessful. The young woman proclaimed that he was her lovyer [*sic*], and moustache was finally obliged to succumb. They met at the guard house. What passed between them is not known, but enough was guessed at to seriously affect the sensibilities of the susceptible young sergeant on duty upon that occasion. After the interview, the young woman started to leave the field, but being overtaken by a real fainting fit, was brought back by a corporal's guard, and a new opportunity was thus afforded the gallant lieutenants at that post to render any assistance which the circumstances might require. Lieut. [Frank H.] Forbes especially signalized himself by his delicate attentions; and it should be mentioned that a large number of other lieutenants signified their willingness to be serviceable in the same direction. "Corporal" is happy to be assured that the young woman is likely to survive her rather doubtful heart-wounds.

Since the above was written, it is rumored that the parties are man and wife.

There is no great harmony in camp upon the subject of music. A proposition to defray the future expense of the Boston Brass Band at the rate of five cents a day per man was not agreed to. Many of us will be sorry to lose the band, which acquits itself very creditably, but we shall have left to us the consolation of Dan Simpson's drum and the veteran Smith's fife.[18] For sixty odd years has the latter been without a peer upon the instrument he uses, and now it does the soul good to hear his trills to *tattoo* and *revielle* [*sic*], as we stand in the company street for roll-call. May he never be without something to wet his whistle!

We received marching orders last Thursday [October 2], and are going to Newbern, N.C., as soon as a transport vessel can be got in readiness. At Newbern it is expected we shall be brigaded under General, now Colonel, Stevenson.[19] This will be gratifying to the regiment.

"Corporal" is requested to correct a statement which crept into his last letter to the effect that private Tucker, of Co. D, was the first to cave in on the late double-quick march to Dedham. It should have read "one of the first." Your correspondent has no desire to sacrifice truth to a pun. Tucker is doubtless a man of bottom [stamina] as well as speed.

Among the testimonials to officers in the 44th should be mentioned the presentation of a sword, sash and belt to Orderly [Charles A.] Cunningham, of Company C, and a sword, sash, belt and pistol to Orderly [Eben R.] Buck of Company B.

Our indefatigable surgeon [Dr. Ware] is organizing and training a corps of assistants who are to lend their aid to the wounded upon the field of battle. The training consists of binding up imaginary wounds, pointing out the position of arteries, showing how to handle fractured limbs, placing men upon litters, and showing how to carry them with the least possible disturbance of the wounded parts.

Since my last the ventilation of the barracks has been improved by sawing out holes in the walls, close to the floors. This is going to the bottom of the matter. The idea of getting rid of carbonic acid gas by forcing it up through the sky-lights is an exploded one, and ought to be forced out of the minds of those who argue that "bad air rise."

Mr. Steffen, formerly a captain in the Prussian service, and recently instructor of the Massachusetts Rifle Club, is a frequent visitor to our regiment, and is now delivering a series of military lessons to our officers. Mr. Steffen is a well educated gentleman, and a military instructor of decided accomplishments.

Since Lieutenant Forbes signalized himself by his gallantry to a distressed fair one, he has figured less agreeably in another affair, and has resigned his commission. His offense appears to have been in putting too much stress upon the subordination due from privates to non-commissioned officers, especially corporals. His language, it must be confessed, was more forcible than elegant, and bordered too strongly upon the profane to escape the censure of Colonel Lee, who asked the lieutenant to resign or submit to a court-martial.

Yesterday and to-day short furloughs have been freely granted, and there is a general impression that they are our last ones. We may not, however, leave for a week or two yet.

Your correspondent notices in the Boston Advertiser the following statement concerning Company F, Captain Storrow, of the 44th Regiment, which was prepared by a member of that company. The men were measured in their stockings, which accounts for the average being somewhat below the common standard. All men are set down as "drinking" who are not conscientiously opposed to the use of ardent spirit in *any form and under all circumstances,* as a beverage:

Of ninety-eight warrant officers and privates, in politics sixty-five were straight Republicans, fourteen conservative Republicans, and three radical Republicans; eleven Union, three Democrats, one Abolitionist, and one undecided.

Thirty-two worship at the Unitarian Church, twenty-one at the Congregationalist, nineteen at the Methodist, fourteen at the Episcopal, eight at the Baptist, and four at the Universalist. Thirty-four are communicants of churches as follows: fourteen of the Methodist church, seven of the Congregational, five of the Episcopal, three of the Unitarian, three of the Baptist, and two of the Universalist.

The average age of the company is thirty-two years seven and seventeen forty-ninths days. The youngest man is seventeen years old, and the oldest forty.

The average height is five feet seven and nine-one hundred and ninety-sixths inches. The shortest man is five feet three and one-quarter inches, the tallest six feet one and one-quarter inches.

The average weight of the company is one hundred and thirty-seven and seventeen forty-ninth pounds. The heaviest man weighs one hundred and sixty-five pounds, and lightest one hundred and fifteen pounds.

Forty-four are set down as drinking; seven as drinking nothing stronger than cider and ale; and forty-seven as not drinking ardent spirits in any shape.

Fifty-seven smoke and forty-four do not; twenty-three neither drink nor smoke; thirty-three both drink and smoke; twenty-four smoke, but do not drink; and eighteen drink, but do not smoke.

There are nine married men and three widowers in the company, and sixteen admit that they are engaged to be married.

The occupations of the company, present and prospective, are as follows:

Thirty-seven intend to be or are merchants; four clergymen, eight lawyers, five farmers, four "literateurs," two physicians, two engineers, two printers, two cabinet makers, two machinists, two musicians, and one of each of the following: chemist, soldier, boot and shoe maker, manufacturer, provision dealer, banker, marble-worker, blacksmith, sailmaker, teabroker, baker, druggist, expressman, jeweler, salesman, bookkeeper; ten are undecided.

There are in the company sixteen graduates and undergraduates, all from Harvard.

In Barracks at Readville,

SATURDAY, OCT. 11, 1862.

The close of another week still finds us

"Down by the Readville farm."

and, with the exception of yesterday and to-day, a glorious week we have had; choice October days, such as call

"the squirrel and the bee
From out their woodland home."

Indian Summer days, fit to inspire poetry in minds most prosaic: a warm sun, an empurpled atmosphere, soft breathing winds, and painted forests to feed the eye withal; glorious moon-lit nights and music to invite visitors; to render charming the duties of the sentinel, "pacing his lonely beat," and to render a healthy life altogether beautiful. A late sunset afforded a spectacle gorgeous as a dream of fairy land. As such a cloud-scene occurs no more than once or twice in a life-time, I cannot forbear to mention the magnificent assembling and coloring of clouds which waited upon the retiring day-king on Tuesday, and impressed every beholder with something of celestial beauty. To live in the midst of such scenes and such surroundings are among the soldier's recompenses. Happy for the soldier if he retains the power to enjoy them!

Wednesday afternoon and evening brought us a host of visitors. The rumors of our near departure brought a perfect cloud of friends. The evening was magnificent, and the tide of social enjoyment ran high. The band discoursed its best music, and our company glee clubs filled the interims quite acceptably. Our leading singers have a large repertory of fine sentimental songs, in addition to a large number of improvisations based upon the "Fourth Battalion" chorus, which runs in this wise:—

"Fourth Battalion,'talion,
Fourth Battalion,'talion,
Fourth Battalion,
Down by the Bigelow farm."

The novelty of our diet has suggested such parodies as the following:

"Ham for breakfast, breakfast,
Ham for breakfast, breakfast,
Ham for breakfast,
Down by the Readville farm.
Ham for dinner, dinner,
Ham for dinner, dinner,
Ham for dinner,
Down by the Readville farm."

And so on for supper. Then again the chorus is varied by substituting the word rice for ham, and with equal effect. Military lessons are sometimes conveyed in the same air, as follows:

"Keep your butts back, butts back,
Keep your butts back, butts back,
Keep your butts back,
Down by the Readville farm."

Then again:

"Thir-teen inches, inches,
Thir-teen inches, inches,
Thir-teen inches,
From breast to back,"

Another favorite route-step song is known as "Saw my leg off," set to an old devotional air, and comprised in these four words, frequently repeated, with the addition of the word "*short*," pronounced in the most abrupt and explosive manner of which human lungs are capable. The effect is rather sublime, as may be imagined.

On Thursday we were treated to a magnificent march over Brush Hill—our first brush. Every inch of the route, which carried us over the most beautiful portion of Milton, and past the residences of the Forbeses, was picturesque as the dream of a poet. Let those who may think this comparison overwrought, pursue the same route one of these fine October days, and then pause to catch the view of sea and landscape from Milton Hill. Our march, which included a distance of fourteen miles, was, considering the state of the atmosphere, the severest of our experience; but it was cheered by the smiles and waving handkerchiefs of beautiful women in windows, gateways, balconies, and groves; and by their more substantial favors in the shape of apples, pears, and cool water. The few men who fell out of the ranks from faintness and exhaustion were of the reputed tougher sort—men of out-door life and pursuits. Your professional men and clerks, clean-limbed and elastic, are the men to endure hardships, all the talk to the contrary notwithstanding. This, I believe, was the observation of the "*Little Corporal.*"

Among the late testimonials in the 44th deserving of mention, are the presentation of a knife, fork, and spoon, in a neat case, to each of the recruits from Framingham, by their friends in that town, and a sword, sash, belt, and various smaller articles of value and convenience, to Orderly [Albert W.] Edmands, of Company A, by his friends in that company.

Your correspondent, and the other members of Company D, are indebted to Corporal [James B.] Gardner for the introduction of a company dog—Romeo, a promising fellow, whose laughing countenance, waving tail, and general intelligence have already won him a host of friends. Several of the boys are industriously laboring to reconcile him to the society of a cat which has come to our barrack.

Mr. Burrage, of the firm of J. M. Beebe & Co., has presented to each member of Company C, Captain Lombard, one of Short's patent box knapsacks. If they can be manufactured in season to supply us before our departure South, the other members of the regiment will probably supply themselves with this knapsack at their own expense, which will amount to $2.50 per man. This knapsack is so adjusted to the shoulders as to be carried with much greater ease than the government article.[20]

At this writing it is generally believed that we shall sail for Newbern about the middle of next week. For particular information on this point, and also with reference to state-rooms and sleeping cars, the public is directed to the Quartermaster's Department, where tickets for such like mythical accommodations are freely dispensed for satisfactory considerations.

By favor of private Geo. W. Sawin, I am this week enabled to give the following statistics of Company D, Captain Sullivan:

Clerks fifty-four, merchants five, farmers four, carpenters two, hotel keepers two, marble workers two, and one each of the following: astronomer, sailor, piano-forte tuner, civil engineer, architect, blacksmith, druggist, glass-blower, jeweller, shoe dealer, surveyor, clergyman, editor, machine stitcher, designer. Seven are under-graduates and one a graduate of Tufts College, one an under-graduate of Harvard and one of Yale. Ninety are single, seven married, and three "engaged." Thirty-three are Unitarians, thirty Universalists, thirteen Orthodox, ten Baptists, three Episcopalians, two Swedenborgians, one Presbyterian, one Methodist, four undecided. Five are church communicants.

Sixty-one are Republicans, and seven ask to be recorded as Abolitionists. The whole sixty-one sustain the emancipation proclamation.[21] There is one "conservative" Republican, thirteen "Union" men, four Douglas Democrats, nine Democrats, and two undecided.

Forty-two do not drink distilled liquors, fifty-five do. The oldest man is aged thirty-three, the youngest eighteen. The average age is twenty-two and two ninety-sevenths. The average height, in shoes, is five feet nine and one-half inches. The tallest man is six feet one inch high; the shortest man five feet three inches. The heaviest man weighs one hundred and eighty-four pounds; the lightest one hundred and fifteen. The average weight is one hundred and forty-two-ninety-sevenths pounds.

Barracks at Readville,

SATURDAY, OCT. 18, 1862.

When in my last I made allusion to our company dog Romeo and his feline companion, we could not foresee the sad and sudden rupture of all the relations between us. On Sunday a fiat from headquarters sent Romeo out of camp; the succeeding night pussy departed this life. Did she die of grief at the loss of Romeo? No one can say; but general opinion inclines to catalepsy. Her little stiffened body was encoffined in a paper box, and placed in the centre of the barrack. A small American flag was thrown over it, and the boys gathering about the remains sung Pleyel's Hymn with an appearance of solemnity that was altogether irresistible. The remains were then carefully placed upon an extemporized bier, and borne to the rear of the kitchen in the midst of a formidable guard of honor, marching with arms reversed, and chanting doleful symphonies. The weeping skies were in sympathy with the occasion; and the clouds were soon shedding tears upon the turf imprisoning the pet of the barrack. Imaginary vollies were fired, but all was *not* over. The funeral party had no sooner returned to the barrack than rumors of foul play began to circulate. A horrid secret was believed to be involved in the death of the cat. Suspicion fell upon a man whose bunk she had lately occupied, and who had been heard to utter threats against pussy for certain alleged rank offenses. The suspected party was arrested, a court organized, the defendant tried, convicted, and sentenced to subsist two days upon the rations. The unhappy man, anticipating his fate, made three desperate attempts to escape, but was foiled in each instance, and forced to submit to the decree of justice.

A large number of the regiment have submitted to [smallpox] vaccination. "Corporal" desires to acknowledge the neat and thorough manner in which our assistant surgeon, Dr. [Theodore W.] Fisher, performed the operation. As the necessity of severe sanitary discipline is becoming apparent to all, the fidelity of Dr. Ware and his assistant are regarded with more favor than at first.

The close resemblance between the life of a soldier in barrack and that of a State Prison convict, regarded in certain outward aspects, affords mingled amusement and disgust. We go for our rations in single file, and with tin mugs and plates. The intercourse between officers and subordinates is scarcely less reserved; and the punishment for small offenses scarcely less severe with the soldier than the prisoner. On inspection days we stand up like well-burnished automata, and are as sensitive to praise or censure regarding the condition of our quarters, guns, &c., as so many children. At our meals and in our bunks we are stared at by visitors just as I remember to have stared at the happy family of "Honorable Gideon Haynes," at Charlestown, on various occasions. When impelled by "sanitary reasons," our keen-eyed surgeons pass through the barracks to see that nothing contraband nestles in the bunks, that the blankets and overcoats are accurately folded, and that only a certain amount of clothing and baggage per man is retained, we stand about and gaze at them just as your readers will remember they were gazed at by the inmates of the House of

Correction which they visited not long ago. On these occasions your correspondent amuses himself by imaginatively regarding private A., with wild hair, as a desperate burglar; private B., of retiring manners, as an incorrigible thief; private L., the gay Lothario, as a heartless deceiver and bigamist; hirsute [hairy] private T., smoking the inevitable briarwood, as a notorious but chivalric foot-pad; privates F., S., &c., of auburn hair, as the persistent incendiaries; and so on.

More princely donations have been made to some of the companies of the 44th regiment. To Co. C, Captain Richardson, Wm. Cumston, Esq., of the firm of Hallett & Cumston, has presented a check for five hundred dollars.

To the same company donations amounting to three hundred dollars, for the purchase of the improved knapsack, have been made by the following gentlemen:

J. M. Beebe & Co., F. Skinner & Co., Alexander Beal, C. W. Cartwright, W. P. Sargent, J. R. Tibbets, Read, Gardner & Co., Wilkinson, Stetson & Co., J. C. Converse & Co., E. & F. King & Co., Horatio Harris, Gorham Roger.[22]

To Co. H, Captain [William] Smith, C. F. Hovey & Co., have presented a full set of the patent knapsacks. Co. K, Captain [Frank W.] Reynolds, have been favored in the same way by a number of friends of that company, and Captain Reynolds has received from the men of his company the gift of a splendid sword. Co. F, Captain Storrow, have received the present of a set of patent knapsacks. The generous donor is too modest to let his name be known, but it is surmised that a young corporal of Co. F, knows all about it.

The wife of Col. Lee has kindly remembered each soldier of the regiment by the gift of a little testimonial card, upon one side of which is printed the Old Hundredth Psalm, and upon the other the name of the recipient written in a neat hand.

On Wednesday we were visited by Governor Andrew and his military family. We received His Excellency with all the honors, and then marched in review. It is believed that better marching and wheelings than those exhibited by the 44th regiment on this occasion have rarely been witnessed by Governor Andrew or any other Governor.

I believe the Governor was accompanied by some members of the Sanitary Commission; but the investigations of that body of gentlemen were nearly confined to the *cuisine* at headquarters.[23] They certainly couldn't be expected to labor upon empty stomachs; but when they had satisfied their hunger, it was too late to see the barracks by day-light. We shall accept the omission as a mark of confidence in the cleanliness and good order of this regiment.

We have had a good share of dismal weather the past week, and have not been allowed the consolation of smoking in the barracks; but the boys have managed to keep the blue devils at bay with mock parades and shows of great effectiveness. One day the camp was electrified by the appearance of an exceedingly well got up elephant, not unprovided with a tail, and waving a trunk of twisted shoddy. Another day we were visited by citizens of Brobdignag [Brobdingnag], ten feet high in their stockings.[24]

Yesterday we made a march of twelve miles through West Roxbury and Dedham. On the way we caught a dim and fleeting glimpse of dear old Boston rising beyond a succession of tree-crowned hills. I remember the scene as a beautiful phantasmagoria [image], such as will come to us in dreams while we encamp upon Southern soil. The march was less delightful than that to Milton Hill. The day was murky, and the air lifeless. There was little to impart zest to the exercise. Sunlight is as important for outdoor physical enjoyment as fresh air, and a soldier makes a mistake in choosing a cloudy day for a march.

We now expect to remain at Readville till the close of the war, except in case Readville is invaded by the enemy, when we shall make a masterly retreat to Mill Village.

To protect us against the strong winds of the inclement season approaching, as well as to impart an air of sylvan beauty to the camp, a dense grove of pine saplings has been planted a little to the South of the barracks. Great praise is due to Lieut. Stebbins, our unwearied chief of police this week, for the well-considered arrangement of this great work.

In The Cars,

I have just time during our run into Boston this morning to say "good bye" to your readers until we arrive at Newbern, N.C. After seven weeks and a half of barrack life at Readville, we at last find ourselves en route for Dixie. To the experience of these seven weeks and a half we shall doubtless many times revert as the poetry of our military experience. There was no little heart in the cheers we gave for the "old camp" as we stood for the last time in the company streets. The old camp at Readville is fraught with pleasant memories of soldierly discipline, of the faithfulness and kindness of our officers, of genial companionship, and a thousand incommunicable pleasures of social life, multiplied and enhanced by the visits and offerings of hosts of friends from Boston and elsewhere.

At our dress parades last evening, after devotional services, our Colonel met a response in the heart of every man in his regiment when he called for three times three for the "good old State and the dear ones we leave behind us." The cheers were given with emphasis; and so were nine others for Col. Lee. "Boys," said the Colonel in response, "I know you meant those cheers for all your officers. Whatever may be your fortune hereafter, rest assured we shall stand by you. Let us all perform our duty to the State and the United States, and may God help us all!" The emotion exhibited by Col. Lee was communicated through the regiment, and there were many wet eyes among soldiers and spectators as we marched back to the barracks.

As soon as practicable, I shall resume this correspondence, confident that it will find readers among the many friends of the 44th in Boston.

CHAPTER 2

En Route to New Bern, North Carolina

On Board Transport Steamer Merrimac,

OCT. 23, 1862.

We lay off Deer Island the night of our embarkation, (last night) and about six o'clock this morning weighed anchor. It was pleasant to sleep one night more so near to dear old Boston, where we knew so many hearts were throbbing at the thought of us. The thousands of lights which came to us in a semi-circle from over the water, seemed like the steady beaming of so many loving eyes, and may be our dreams were the sweeter for the fancy. Don't imagine, however, that we all slept as quietly as we did in those luxurious bunks at Readville. The 44th Regiment occupies the lower deck of the Merrimac, and has already had a decided flavor of life in the steerage. Here we are, "the flower" (or flour) "of the youth of Boston," (*vide* Boston Journal of October 23), packed like so many herrings in the steerage. Our bunks are not half as good as those at Readville, and, sad to say, we haven't enough even of these. They afford us little more than space enough in which to turn over. Here and there we are afforded a small glimmer of light from the deck, and a little fresh air by devious channels. Into the bunk of your correspondent it happens to come in an unpleasantly strong current, as if to rebuke his former passionate professions of love for fresh air under more favorable circumstances, or as a piece of retributive justice for opening doors and windows against the protests of tender comrades.

The five hundred men of the Third Regiment who accompany us, and who are known by their black overcoats as the "men in mourning," are better commoded [*sic*] between decks, one story above us. They will do, but as for ourselves, as we lie stretched out here in this dark, reptile sort of existence, we are fain to ask ourselves if we are really intelligent beings with souls; if the "flower" has really come to this; if the "pet of many a household," (*vide* Boston Transcript of Oct. 22) has really been reduced to treatment no better than that of the poorest emigrant. But we ought not to grumble while scores of our regiment are obliged to stretch themselves upon the cold deck, upon the hatches, passage ways, &c.; and we do *not* grumble. Your correspondent only gives *facts*. He, like many others, *expected* to "rough it," and rather likes it.

Our breakfast this morning was a mug of very muddy coffee, and a piece of bread. For dinner we were afforded boiled beef and potatoes and coffee, but no bread. We could get along better with this but for occasional tantalizing sights and smells of poultry and puddings and garden vegetables which grace the cabin tables. Our officers confess that they live like fighting cocks, but they should have the credit of sincerely commiserating our unavoidable treatment. O, genial-hearted lobster-man of the rubicund [ruddy] face and Pickwickian[1] aspect, who rose to bless us in Commercial street, could you but waft us one fish from your shelly store, we know how much good it would do you and us; but tonight, alas, we were forced to sup on bread and water, with a dessert of aggravating conversation about porter house steaks, cold chicken, warm biscuit, etc., etc. If we live we will have our revenge some day at Parker's goodly hostelry.

FRIDAY, OCT. 24.

It is said that we made sixteen miles an hour last night, running ninety-six miles in six hours. We have passed Montauk Light, and at this writing (between eight and nine o'clock) we are supposed to be somewhere off the Jersey shore. Our consort, the Mississippi, has been in sight over our starboard quarter all the morning. Thus far the weather has been extremely favorable, but we have not all escaped the misery of sea-sickness— a malady which must have been aggravated by our close, ill-ventilated quarters, and the unavoidable filth attending the herding together of fifteen hundred men on shipboard. Scarcely a breath of air was stirring last night, and very little came down to our bunks. After remaining on deck a few moments this morning, an attempt to penetrate to our quarters induced a nausea which we found impossible to endure, and so we incontinently rushed upon deck to swallow our rations, without the intervention of spoon or plate. We were first served to a large piece of bread and a mug of coffee, and then to parboiled rice, which rattled upon our plates. O, Readville rations, bad as you might have been, may the tongue that utters aught against you cleave to the roof of the slanderer's mouth. It is expected we are to have beef for dinner, as several noble quarters were not long since dragged along close by the rear of the horses' stalls, on their way to the boilers, where they were set to cooking without washing.

We wish our friends could see us at meal times. We are a study for an artist at those interesting periods. We are obliged to eat on the upper deck. One fellow is seen burying his nose in a loaf of bread, another gnaws a beef bone until his face is resplendant [sic] with grease; but the colored boy of the color company, making his dinner from a mass of fat and gristle, is the observed of all observers. His face shines like varnished ebony, but he is still intent upon his greasy repast, and oblivious to the smiles and jeers of the amused spectators who surround him. Feed away, juvenile Ethiop, woolly headed Mark Tapley, may nothing come between you and jolliness forever.[2]

This afternoon we were signalled by the Mississippi, when she came up to within hailing distance. Hearty cheers were exchanged between the swarms on the decks of either steamer. We were glad to notice on board the Mississippi one lieutenant and a number of non-coms, whom the Merrimac had unfortunately left behind. As night shuts in we are supposed to be off Fortress Monroe. We have a balmy atmosphere and a brisk wind from the west. Hundreds of the boys have stretched themselves for sleep upon the upper deck.

SATURDAY, OCT. 25.

This morning we are supposed to be steaming along between Fortress Monroe and Cape Hatteras. The sea is smooth, and the genial breath of the South is upon us. We feel as if Spring-time had come upon us suddenly, and those not afflicted with sea-sickness feel good this morning. The Mississippi is just ahead of us.

On board these two steamers are three thousand soldiers with arms and accoutrements. We are the same as defenceless. From our vast navy of war vessels not even one little gunboat has been spared to escort us to our destination, and this in the face and eyes of the fact that a number of formidable rebel privateers are scouring the seas and scattering destruction in their path. Is there any apology for such risk and negligence? We cannot see it.

As the weather becomes soft, genial and glorious upon deck, our situation below grows more intolerable. It is almost impossible to exaggerate the uncomfortable, unhealthy character of our quarters upon the lower deck. A prison dungeon is not worse supplied with air and sunlight; and to make matters still worse, the ship has but a miserable supply of lanterns at night. It is to be acknowledged that there are a few feeble devices for sending air below, but they are altogether inadequate. With the splendid machinery on board this steamer, it would be an easy matter by the use of fans to thoroughly ventilate every portion of the ship. In the course of another century, ship-builders will learn, as house-builders are now learning, that means must be employed for the introduction of a plenty of fresh air into all structures where men are herded together. We cannot be too thankful that the weather has been so favorable since we left Boston. A thousand sick men in such quarters as these would have made a hell afloat. Now I would like to speak a good word for the ship. She is staunch, steady, swift and well officered. She has carried twenty-three hundred men, but only a thousand and [in?] comfort can dwell together upon her decks. The few who get a chance to wash their hands and faces are obliged to do so in salt water. It is reported that Capt. Sampson was quite thunder-struck by a request of our officers that he would afford us means of daily ablutions, and that he remarked we were the first regiment he ever carried who had expressed a desire to wash their hands and faces.

Our "holy friars," the black-coated men of the 3d regiment, appear to be a good set of fellows, and we all get along most amicably together. Col. [Silas P.] Richmond and Major [John] Morrissey accompany this half of the regiment.

We have been thoughtfully regaled with an apple apiece a day, and they have proved wonderfully refreshing, especially as we are allowed but two meals a day on shipboard. Now, when we most need a sutler, no sutler is to be seen, although at rare intervals we can buy hard apples at five cents apiece, and cake at fifty cents a pound. Last evening Co. F were regaled with a dish of tea by some Good Samaritan, said to be Capt. Storrow, who is highly praised for his careful attention to the men of his command. I wish to bear similar testimony in behalf of the officers of Co. D, Capt. Sullivan and Lieuts. Blake and Stebbins.

I wish my fun-loving readers could have stood at the hatchway between decks this morning, and seen the soldiers slide down the slippery stairs. Some carried mugs of coffee with no other apparent object than to pour the beverage upon the heads and shoulders of those who preceded them. The libation was not greatly enjoyed except by a crowd of spectators at the foot of the stairs, who hailed every accident and discomfiture of the sort with shouts of laughter.

At 9 o'clock this morning we are in near view of the North Carolina coast, and doubtless very near Beaufort. Last night, like all the weather during the voyage, was delightful, and the long upper deck was literally packed with sleepers lying at every possible angle and posture, with arms and legs affectionately crossed and interlocked. The general health of the men remains excellent.

Eleven o'clock finds us at the wharf at Morehead City, near Beaufort, and making preparations for a speedy landing in the midst of a drizzling rain.

This letter is written without conveniences, and under the most miserable and disagreeable circumstances.

We are soon to take the cars for Newbern. You will hear from me there.

CHAPTER 3

New Bern

Newbern, N.C.,

OCT. 26, 1862.

When we stepped from the decks of the Merrimac we were provided with shelter from a drizzling rain in the depot of the railroad connecting Morehead with Newbern; and while there we made the structure ring with patriotic and devotional songs—our first salute to Dixie. We were conveyed from Morehead to Newbern on platform cars, and were, of course, entirely exposed to the weather. We had scarcely got under way before there set in a violent rain, which continued almost without intermission until our arrival at Newbern. Our garments, of course, were thoroughly drenched, but, nevertheless, the trip was highly enjoyed. The mild and invigoring [*sic*] pine breezes of the old North State contrasted so deliciously with the foetid atmosphere and filth of the steamer, that even a drenching rain was insufficient to quench our exhilaration of spirits. A more miserable and worthless tract of country than the barren pine region which we traversed cannot well be imagined, so that under all the circumstances of the trip, our lively frame of mind may be regarded as quite Mark Tapleyish.[1] Pickets from the Massachusetts 27th regiment were scattered along the road at frequent intervals. We cheered them, and they cheered us. Some of them were sheltered by tents, others in cabins, and some in substantial log structures calculated for defence. Occasional negro villages, and scattering negro huts were objects of lively interest. All hands turned out to see us as we shot past. The men showed their entire ivory, and the women threw their black arms up and down in the most vehement approbation. We also witnessed several good specimens of the real Southern "white trash." The country is well calculated to develop this species of the genus homo. The women are the most doleful and disgusting looking of their sex. We suspected all of them of looking secesh [rebel] daggers at us. A few did cheer us on after a fashion, waving their arms up and down—a sort of melancholy God-speed. We doubt if they possessed a solitary white handkerchief, or any other white textile fabric proper to be displayed on such occasions. We once stopped to water the iron horse close by a field of sweet potatoes growing within some rebel breastworks erected to command the railroad. The proprietor of the potato patch came forth with his wife and children and presented us several handsful of the vegetables, for which they were rewarded with vociferous cheers as the train rolled on.

At dusk we crossed the river Neuse, and found ourselves in the pretty little city of Newbern, where, as may be guessed, we received a hearty welcome from the Massachusetts men stationed at this place. Our friends, the contrabands, were not the least enthusiastic of those who welcomed us.[2] We were quartered for the night in a spacious machine shop, well lighted with gas. We have just supped upon hard bread and codfish broiled upon a forge. An attempt was made to supply us with coffee, but it miserably failed, and your correspondent is one of a respectable number who go to bed without the soldier's chiefest bodily consolation. As he closes his record of the day the air in the machine shop is thick with hard bread and flying codfish sent from invisible hands.

Our men are scattered about town this morning, luxuriating upon such breakfasts as can be purchased with money. They are constantly coming in with beaming faces and tantalizing narrations of what they got to eat. Your correspondent only strayed a few steps from the engine house before he found a little cabin where a neat colored woman served him with two kinds of hoe-cake, roasted sweet potatoes, and sage tea.

We have not been in Newbern long enough to give you much news. Barracks are erecting here, it is reported, for fifteen thousand soldiers. Ours are not yet completed. Among the regiments at Newbern and vicinity are the Massachusetts 17th, 23d, 24th, 25th, 27th, and 44th. The 3d and 5th, which were detained at Morehead City by the grounding of the Mississippi, will probably arrive here to-day.

Newbern, N.C.,

WEDNESDAY, OCT. 29, 1862.

We are encamped upon the western bank of the river Neuse, about one-third of a mile to the north of the city of Newbern. Monday night most of the regiment passed in tents, a few rods from here. Yesterday we were industriously employed in ditching and smoothing the ground around our cloth-houses, laying floors, constructing fire places and chimneys, and had just got things in the most satisfactory condition, when Company D was ordered to strike tents and go into the half-completed barrack which we now occupy conjointly with the carpenters and a great quantity of loose lumber. In a very short time all our companies will be comfortably housed, unless unexpected orders intervene. The barracks of each regiment are continuous—occupying one long building. They are provided with windows and more commodious bunks than those at Readville. Our easterly windows look out upon the Neuse. On the other side the barrack is shaded with cedar trees. To the west of us is encamped the Connecticut Tenth Regiment, a Rhode Island Battery, and the New York Third Artillery Regiment. A New York cavalry regiment is also encamped in the vicinity. These are all additional to the troops in this department mentioned in my last letter. The Connecticut Tenth, although much reduced in numbers and effectiveness, has greatly surprised us new comers by the excellency of their manual drill. It is almost equal to that of the Chicago Zouaves.[3]

The men of the old regiments at Newbern are not inclined to regard the nine months' men with much favor, and indulge in a good many taunts having reference to bounty money and good clothes. They take great pleasure in assuring us that General [John G.] Foster proposed to give us a full nine months' work, and that we need not expect to escape the warmest part of the business before us. They are considerably disgusted with our unveteran-like ways, and furnish us with innumerable suggestions. The bugles, numbers, &c., upon our caps, they regard as vanity. They allow no "cullured pusson" to wear Uncle Sam's buttons, and it is now rumored that those of our boys who shall appear in the streets of Newbern with "infantry" buttons will find themselves suddenly minus those articles. The soldier who returns the salute of a negro is set down as a transgressor of military etiquette, and privates who salute each other are laughed at.

The remarks of one of our boys that "there is nothing but niggers and soldiers in Newbern," well describes the impression of your correspondent. Most of the resident secesh skedaddled long ago, and as others become unearthed, and refuse to take the oath, they are conveyed beyond the Union lines. Many white residents, professedly Union, are believed to be playing possum.

The first night we spent in Newbern is said to have been the coldest of the season up to that time. Monday night and Tuesday morning also seemed very much like late October days in New England, and required about the same number of woollen blankets and overcoats as are requisite at home now-a-days. We are cautioned to be out but little in the evening, and to wear overcoats after five o'clock. We are also very earnestly cautioned to drink but little water, and to eat sparingly of negro "chicken fixins" in the shape of sweet potatoes, pies and cakes, which contrabands bring into camp in great profusion.

We are no sooner comfortably settled in barracks than word comes to us of an immediate march into the interior of the State, perhaps to Kinston, perhaps to Swansbororough [*sic*], which are in possession of the rebels.[4] At all events we are doubtless bound to extend our lines, and we now have the troops to do it with, although we scarcely expected that General Foster would put us in motion quite so speedily as this.

The health of the regiment is excellent, everything considered.

Lieutenant Blake, of Company D, has been detailed to act upon the staff of Colonel Stevenson, commanding our brigade. We thus lose an invaluable officer from our company. Lieutenant Stebbins, who succeeds Lieut. Blake, is one of the most faithful and considerate officers in the regiment, and will make the place of Lieutenant Blake good.

CHAPTER 4

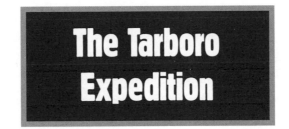

The Tarboro Expedition

Washington, N.C.,

OCT. 31, 1862.

As remarked in my last letter from Newbern, we had no sooner got comfortably ensconced in our splendid new barracks than we received orders to join one of the largest military expeditions which has been known in North Carolina for many a day. The expedition consists of nearly all the available force at Newbern and vicinity, infantry, artillery and cavalry, and cannot fall much below ten thousand men, most of whom left Newbern early yesterday morning, on board steam transports, and schooners propelled by tugs, under the command of Major-General Foster.

We were in what is called light marching order; but our two blankets, haversacks containing three days' rations of hard bread, beef, coffee and sugar, canteens, equipments and rifles, made up a very considerable load.

After about thirty hours of slow steaming down the Neuse, through Pamlico Sound and up the Tar river, we disembarked at Washington, one of the bastard "cities" of North Carolina.[1] A journey more tame in its surroundings can scarcely be imagined. The shores of the two rivers present an almost unbroken level; and the monotony of a stunted growth of trees is barely interrupted by the habitations of man. In places the trees have a beautiful coloring, which reminded us of the October woods in New England, and there is a sort of lonesome grandeur in the broad streams themselves.

Washington looks like Newbern. Some of the streets are prettily shaded, and there are a few elegant residences. At a window of one of the latter we espied a pretty young white woman playing a piano. Besides these, having been here only a couple of hours or so, I saw little but "niggers and soldiers," a phrase which also describes Newbern. We were marched through the town into a breezy field on the shore of the Tar river, where we stacked arms, made fires, and boiled our coffee. Finding ourselves in the vicinity of a row of negro shanties, the board fences surrounding them were soon converted into fuel and shelter. The shanties were then besieged by our hungry boys, and the black "aunties" and their daughters were soon driving a good business in supplying the soldiers with hoe-cake.[2]

The vociferous demands of the boys to be supplied in their turn were quite confusing to the accommodating cooks, who mixed their meal and water and transferred it to iron pans with the rapidity of experts in the business. Each fire-place was surrounded by hungry expectants, some of whom, to make sure of their cakes, drew their initials in the yielding dough, and then stood by like watch-dogs until the tempting morsel was browned and "soaked" to the point of perfection. "Soaked" is a word of the cook, and describes the finishing process. The venerable proprietor of one of the shanties remarked that he was glad to see the Yankees, but this was the second time they had torn down his fence.

Washington is reputed to be a "Union city."[3] In the language of one of the inhabitants, "There was a right smart of Union here before the proclamation, but now it is the other way." It's of no consequence, as Toots says. The North Carolina [Union] First Regiment is here.

EVENING.—We bivouac to-night upon the northerly shore of the Tar River. The field is covered with extemporized shelters of rude but ingenious construction, and are supplied with generous beds of cornhusks. Some sugar-box shooks in the vicinity have been levied upon, and some of the boys are literally boxing themselves up.[4] Others have stretched their rubber blankets for shelter. Some have constructed shanties of boards. Our woollen blankets have been voted an incumbrance, and are packed away. For the lively work now in prospect we must per force carry lighter loads than we brought from Newbern; and although we shall miss the blankets o'nights, we shall miss them more [less?] upon our wearisome marches when every ounce weighs a pound.

I cannot tell you what we are going to do. There is supposed to be work enough, especially as it is reported that fifteen thousand rebel troops are in North Carolina, and some of them at no great distance from this point. We may next be heard from at Kinston or Williamston.

On Board Transport Steamer Geo. Collins, From Plymouth to Newbern, N.C.

TUESDAY, NOV. 11, 1862.

Your correspondent finds himself one of a large expeditionary corps en route back to Newbern, after one of the longest and severest marches in the history of the present war. Since the date of my last, which was written at Washington, at the head of Pamlico Sound, the regiment has led rather an active and stirring life for a regiment only about sixty days old. We left Washington early Sunday morning, Nov. 2d, marching northward that day nearly twenty miles, with nothing to break the monotony save a light brush with the enemy's picket a few miles out of town. We bagged one or two of their horses, and soon passed their bivouac, where a rebel blanket and some other articles were burning. Here the road forked, and upon the left the smoke of a burning bridge showed that the rebels were making good their escape. At noon we halted near the plantation of a decently to-do farmer. A son of the farmer was observed to wear rebel buttons, and he was taken prisoner. There was then little doubt as to the rebel proclivities of the old man (a good tow-headed, blear-eyed specimen of white trash,) whose premises were pretty thoroughly searched for the means of providing dinner and other refreshments. Sweet potatoes, apple brandy, honey, &c., helped the boys' rations amazingly, and these delicacies were relished the more because they were taken along with several rebel weapons of death. The female portion of the family sat upon the piazza and gazed upon the soldiers with a sort of stolid fear depicted upon their faces. They were tolerably good looking, and one of them wore a quiet, venerable aspect, which moved our respect and sympathy. At dusk we stirred up a secesh hornets' nest, and a lively battle of musketry was heard in front. As we hurried forward Gen. Foster sat with his staff at a bend in the road, and smilingly informed us that there were "only seven or eight hundred of them." Just before this our two right flank companies, H and C, Capts. Smith and Lombard, were detached from the regiment and sent forward as skirmishers.

Proceeding by the road they descended a hill and entered a piece of woods through which ran a considerable stream of water. They had no sooner entered the water at the fording-place than they were fired upon by a considerable force of rebel infantry in ambuscade; but our men bravely stood their ground, and replied promptly to the fire.[5] After a few rounds, the guns and ammunition became useless from wetting, when companies H and C were withdrawn, although not until they had crossed the ford. Companies E and I, Captains Spencer Richardson and [Joseph R.] Kendall, were sent forward. Company I was held in reserve, while E succeeded in passing the ford and ascended to the summit of a hill on the opposite side, but not without brisk skirmishing, receiving and returning several volleys, and capturing three prisoners. One of these was taken by private Michael Parsons under circumstances so creditable to his pluck that Parsons was promoted to a sergeantry.

General John G. Foster and his staff, New Bern, North Carolina, 1863. Courtesy of the Southern Historical Collection, University of North Carolina at Chapel Hill (Herman Biggs Papers).

After Company E, the stream was crossed by the Connecticut 10th regiment, Colonel Pettiborn. The ford being thus thoroughly commanded, word was sent to the rear, and the entire column moved forward, the 44th regiment passing the Connecticut 10th, thus giving to the Massachusetts 44th the honor of the next advance. Having attained the summit of the hill previously occupied by Company E, the 44th deployed on either side of the road, and allowed the Massachusetts 24th to pass to the front. The advance was again resumed, and we entered a piece of dense woods. Here we felt our way cautiously, once halting for a considerable space of time. The moon shone brightly, scattering the light through the scarcely moving branches. The voices of birds and the hum of insects filled the air with tones eloquent of summer at the North. The world looked too beautiful for strife and slaughter. Here we sunk down upon the ground, almost overcome by the fatigue of a day's severe march, and were with difficulty restrained from falling into a deep sleep. We were soon aroused by the order to advance, and proceeded cautiously about half a mile farther, the road skirting, for a portion of the distance, an open field on our left. Just at the extremity of this field we were again fired upon from the hedge. This hazardous kind of advancing was then wisely abandoned, and the column filed into the field, under the cover of Belger's splendid artillery, which having assumed a commanding position, shelled the rebel ambuscade in magnificent style. Sweeter music than the music of *those* spheres, whistling their way into the nest of cowardly traitors, never fell upon mortal ears. From our observation of the rapid and well-directed fire, we were not surprised to hear, as we did subsequently, that many a rebel bit the dust on the morning of the third of November, at "Chopper's Creek, near Rawle's Mill," which will stand for the name of this affair.

At the ford the casualities [*sic*] of the 44th consisted of the following:

Company E. Killed—Charles Morse. Wounded—Charles E. Roberts.

Company C. Killed—Charles Rollins. Slightly wounded—Sergeant Pond, William A. Smallidge. Lieutenant [James W.] Briggs was momentarily stunned by the near passing of a projectile, but speedily recovered.

Company H. Killed—none. Wounded—Richard V. Depeyster, left arm amputated; [Augustus] Jacobs, of South Scituate, in the back (severe); Harrison Parker, 2d, in right arm (slightly).

At the place where we were last fired on, Lieutenant Stebbins, of Company D, while assisting in rallying the men of his company, was slightly wounded in one of his legs, and had his garments perforated in several places.

It is doubtful if the history of the war furnishes an instance where a skirmish with the enemy has occurred under circumstances more trying to the Union troops, or better calculated to test their moral endurance and pluck. A regiment only sixty days old altogether, without experience in battle, was called upon at the close of a day's severe march to encounter a deadly foe in ambuscade, upon ground of their own selection, at a long, deep ford, and in dense, dark woods; but I am happy to record the testimony of all observers that the officers and men of the 44th Regiment exhibited a gallantry and fearlessness befitting veterans themselves, and sufficient to gain expressions of admiration from the old regiments in the expedition, who had previously regarded us with, to draw it mildly, an over-critical eye, regarding us as more ornamental than useful.

Some of the last companies of the 44th to cross the ford were for several minutes under the fire of two rebel cannon planted on an eminence to our right. Grape and shell fell on either side of us in a lively manner, but, most fortunately, without injury to us. Before entering the ford a shower of bullets passed close over our heads as we lay in the road. Our recumbent position at this point, as well as at the last place of attack, doubtless saved us from considerable loss of life.

It was two hours past midnight before we received orders to bivouac, when we sunk down and slept upon our arms in the open air. It was a cold, damp night, and after a few hours' sleep, we awoke wet, cold and stiff, the combined effects of half an hour's bath in the stream the previous night, a heavy North Carolina dew, and the fatigue of the former day's march. When we opened our eyes we discovered that the field was traversed by a formidable rebel earthwork, of which our rapid advance had prevented the completion.

At an early hour Monday morning the column resumed its forward movement, and reached Williamston, a pretty town on the Roanoke river, where we were glad to find several of our gunboats and a lot of extra rations for our troops. Here we rested, foraged, dined and made ourselves extremely comfortable for a couple of hours or so. The white residents had skedaddled, and we entered into possession of their horses, mules, wagons, pigs, poultry and honey. From Williamston we advanced about five miles and bivouacked in a cornfield. On our route thither we were delayed two hours by the destruction of a bridge. Tuesday we dined at Hamilton, another town on the Roanoke, about the size of Williamston, where we again fared luxuriously upon the products of the country. In the evening we advanced beyond Hamilton about three miles, and encamped again in a cornfield. I regret to say that we left Hamilton by the light of several burning houses, which were said to have been fired by some soldiers in retaliation for the shooting of a Union soldier by a rebel picket near the town. The firing of the buildings was generally condemned as unnecessary and outrageous.

Wednesday, after a further advance of about a dozen miles, we halted for dinner upon the road to Tarboro'. After dinner we retraced our steps a couple of miles, and took a road to the right in the direction of Halifax, which we pursued until midnight through a miserable swampy territory before we found a place fit for an encampment. Here we bivouaced in rain and mud within six or seven miles of Tarboro', a reputed rebel stronghold having railroad communication with Weldon and Richmond. When we arose Thursday morning we were confidently expecting to march upon Tarboro', and were not a little surprised to find ourselves turning backward. Then came rumors thick and fast of a largely augmented rebel force at Tarboro', and of a design to cut off our retreat at the swamp in the event of our retreat.

When the columns changed roads on Wednesday, two companies of our regiment, A and G, Captains James Richardson and [Charles] Hunt, together with two pieces of cannon and a small force of cavalry, all under the command of the Major of the New York 3d cavalry, were sent forward upon the direct route for the purpose, as it is supposed, of diverting the attention of the rebels from a proposed attack in the rear. The plan, however, if such was the plan, did not succeed. The little force soon found itself opposed to a formidable enemy in ambuscade, and after a somewhat brisk skirmish, in which one of our mounted pickets was killed, concluded it would be wise to rejoin our main force, which they did the next morning at day-light, at our encampment, after a forced and very fatiguing march, and, for a portion of the distance, upon the double quick.

Whatever may have been the truth regarding the rebel force in our vicinity, certain it is that we made a very rapid march back to Hamilton—a march which tested the endurance of our troops in no small degree—the more because of the uncomfortable weather and muddy condition of the roads. Never was the shelter of real houses more welcome than to our jaded troops when they arrived at Hamilton on Thursday night. We entered into possession of the deserted buildings, and were soon basking in the genial warmth streaming from a hundred fire-places—a warmth mingled with the savory odors of cooking meats and vegetables. Some of the companies fell upon quarters almost luxurious. All were thankful for any kind of shelter. In the morning we were a little surprised to find the ground white with snow, and conjectured that the "Sunny South" was ahead of Massachusetts in that particular, for once.

On Friday we marched to Williamston, where we tarried until Sunday morning, and recruited our strength by rest and comfortable fare. Here we hoped to take transports for Newbern, but were destined for one more day's march, and Sunday night we encamped near Plymouth, after a quick march of nearly twenty miles. Monday noon we embarked for Newbern on board this steamer [the *George Collins*], having in tow a schooner with a portion of the regiment. We are in a gratified frame of mind. Why should we not be? We have succeeded in effecting a march of full one hundred miles through the enemy's country; we have been under fire, and are said to have stood it in a creditable manner; the endurance of our troops has been tested as it never was before by the troops in North Carolina, and a green regiment has been found as capable of performing a severe march as the veterans of Roanoke and Newbern.[6] In fact fewer men of the 44th fell out of the ranks from fatigue than those of any other regiment in the three brigades composing the expedition. It must be confessed, however, that the old regiments do not give us any extra credit for this endurance, but say we *ought* to march well, coming as we do so recently from home, in good health, and before we have been subjected to the hardships and sickness incident to the soldier. There is, no doubt, much truth in this; but it is almost a question whether our advantages of condition are not offset by the seasoning and experience of men a year in the field before us. Moreover, and chiefly, we have reason to feel satisfied with the expedition, forasmuch as Gen. Foster says its object was accomplished. What that object was is not well known at this writing; but it may have been the diversion of rebel troops from Weldon, or Richmond, to aid General [John A.] Dix on the one hand, or General [George B.] McClellan on the other.[7] We certainly succeeded in cleaning the rebel troops out of a large part of North Carolina, and in giving them a terrible scare.

Our impressions of North Carolina have not been rendered more favorable by a more thorough acquaintance. Most of the territory we traversed is a dead, uninteresting level, thinly populated in times of peace, and almost depopulated by the war. We passed considerable growing cotton, and very many large fields of unharvested corn. We met a few white people, but scarcely a Union man or woman, even professedly. At Hamilton we found one gratifying exception in the person of a venerable man nearly eighty years of age, who welcomed us with emotion and bid us a regretful "good bye." He had a son in the rebel army—forced there by the conscription, after escaping three drafts. We sung several patriotic songs to the old man, who listened to us with uncovered head and streaming eyes, and bowed his grateful acknowledgements. There were few who witnessed the scene who did not share the old man's emotion. We left him with cheers and blessings, and felt our patriotism renewed by the interview.

Above Hamilton we passed a negro village, the residents of which assembled along the road to cheer us on.[8] Their spokesman was an old colored man, who kept repeating, as the column passed along, *"We've long wished you well, but we daren't show it!"* This, too, was an inspiration to us, as was also the crowd of poor blacks following in our train wherever we moved, under a vague presentiment that the day of their redemption had come, and that liberty was in store for them.

Our friends will inquire as to what condition we find ourselves at the close of so severe a march. There are a few who have been placed upon the sick list in consequence of the severity of our experience, some of whom were sent to Newbern by gunboats from Hamilton when we first arrived there, and others to Plymouth by the same means, upon our return. There are many sore and bleeding feet which have worn out their shoes and stockings. Nearly all of us have lost several pounds of superfluous flesh, and some are quite gaunt and hirsute [hairy], not to say dirty. As a regiment, contrasted with our appearance at Readville, we may be said to look decidedly rough. Not a little of the "sacred soil" adheres to the late spotless blue of our habiliments. Grease spots and smut variegate our coats and pantaloons, which in some cases present large openings made by lying too closely to the camp fires. We would march twenty miles for the sake of exhibiting ourselves to our friends in Washington street as we look to-day.

A large army passing through an enemy's country presents a grand and formidable appearance to a novitiate like your correspondent, and it also presents features of a grotesque comicality scarcely less striking. As we advanced, our teams elongated with great rapidity. Every stray or deserted vehicle along our route, from a carryall to a handcart, and every horse and mule possessing the slightest power of locomotion, was pressed into our service. Some of the teams thus extemporised, and laden or driven by sick and disabled soldiers and contraband servants, would have done credit to any turn-out of the antiques and horribles [in Boston]. Some poor mules were literally covered with a burden of humanity equal to their own bulk. Many of our baggage wagons were drawn by mules, and at night their unmusical voices seemed raised in solemn protest against the hardships and abuse heaped upon their race.

Various instances of foraging, although not so funny to one party interested, were among the amusing episodes of our progress through North Carolina. It was not a little entertaining to see some of our boys, now in hot pursuit of half-frantic poultry and pigs, and wildly beating the air in the vicinity of bee-hives which they had ruthlessly overturned in an irrepressible passion for stored sweets. The sight and taste of that white honey-comb will not soon pass from the memory of our jaded and hungry soldiers! Nor you, apple-jack, beverage of the South, cheering *and* inebriating, welcome substitute for whisky rations.

"Here's to good old apple-jack,
Drink her down;
Here's to good old apple-jack,
Drink her down;
Here's to good old apple-jack,
It will lay you on your back,
Drink her down,
Drink her down!"

"Corporal" is not responsible for this. It was wafted to his ears from the quarter deck of the transport.

Newbern,
NOV. 14, 1862.

We arrived here this morning. I had more to say, but have no time to say it before the close of the mail.

Newbern, N.C.,
NOV. 15, 1862.

By the last mail I sent you a hurried account of our recent expedition to the vicinity of Tarborough. Time was not afforded me to say all I desired to, nor all that would have been gratifying to the many friends of the 44th at home, who have to turn to the Herald for a connected account of our adventures.

What I wished to say in my previous letter, which, by the way, I hope escaped the Newbern censorship, and which I would say now, if it would not be unmilitary, was a word about one high in command in this regiment, who has more than met the sanguine expectations of those who knew him intimately as one apt to command, prompt in expedients, cool and collected in danger, tender-hearted to the sick and disabled, generous in all his promptings. The late trying experiences of the regiment enable me to speak unqualifiedly upon these points. It would also gratify your correspondent if he might be allowed to bear testimony to the high qualities of other field and staff officers, and to personally acknowledge the considerate kindness of those who had kind words and kinder acts for the sick, weary and foot-sore during our late severe march through the enemy's country. To one of our captains great praise is awarded for his unwavering endurance and pluck throughout the march; the more as he had no sooner arrived at Washington, N.C., than he was deprived of his first Lieutenant, (detailed to act upon the staff of Colonel Stevenson, commanding our brigade,) and a day or two afterward, of his remaining Lieutenant, who was forced to return to Newbern in consequence of a wound received at the skirmish of Chopper's Creek. The manner in which the Captain alluded to, inexperienced in campaigning, and almost unaided, sustained his command, and kept his men together during the eight days' march, give him a new hold upon the cordial respect of his company and superior officers.[9]

You can suppose that we were glad to get back into comfortable barracks at Newbern, where we received a cordial and affectionate welcome from the Cripple Reserve and Home Guard, who had kept watch and ward over our knapsacks and made themselves comfortable, while we made eighteen miles a day and glory. But they wouldn't allow us to patronize them. *They* had seen service. Our pickets were driven in a night or two before, the long-roll had sounded over Newbern, and the Home Guard were actually called out.[10] It seems that a force of rebels, under the supposition that our garrison was essentially weakened by the reconnaisance, came down to feel of our strength, but wisely concluded not to come too near, although succeeding in killing two of our picket guard, belonging to the Massachusetts 24th. I should have mentioned in my previous letter that a member of this regiment was shot at Chopper's Creek the same night we lost two men from the 44th. By the way, we have just received from a Richmond paper an account of this skirmish, by which we learn for the first time that one of our cavalry companies was annihilated, and that our general loss was very severe, while the rebels lost but two men killed and a few wounded. Per contra, veracious contrabands at Williamston told us of wagon-loads of rebels slain and wounded carried through that place. We thought [Captain James] Belger's battery was doing the business for them, and were quite prepared for the report given by the negroes.[11]

The Newbern Progress, which is published under the supervision of the military authorities here, gives the following account of our expedition:

> Federal Reconnaisance to Hamilton.—On the 3d inst., Major-General Foster, with about five thousand men, made a reconnaisance in force from Washington, N.C., towards Weldon, with the intention of taking Williamston and Hamilton, which points were strongly fortified by intrenchments, and also to interrupt the reported construction of iron-clads on the Roanoke River.[12] The expedition advanced overland for some distance without meeting an enemy. The rebels, about three thousand strong, made a stand, however, at a place called Little Creek, but were repulsed with slight loss.
>
> Our troops pushed on to Williamston and Hamilton, where they executed a flank movement, with a fair prospect of bagging the whole rebel force, who, however, saved themselves by a hasty flight. The rebel fortifications about these places, which were more than three miles in length, and of a very formidable character, were destroyed by our troops. No iron-clads were found. The places taken were not garrisoned by General Foster, inasmuch as the rebels can be whipped out of them again at any time.

Last evening we were delighted to welcome the Massachusetts 45th and other regiments, by the Merrimac, Mississippi and Saxon. We regaled them with coffee, and listened with astonishment to their narrations of snow and sleighing in Boston last Sunday. The letters and papers they brought us, and which came by mail and one subsequent arrival, were inexpressibly welcome, and were devoured with even more avidity than our rations at the close of a day's march.

To-day the 44th underwent its first inspection by General Foster. Of course we put our best foot forward. Leather and brass and steel shone as they had not shone before since they left Readville. Spotless white handkerchiefs and gloves in the hands of the General's aids [sic] sought for soiling matter about our rifles, but generally without success. The General was pleased to compliment us. He was accompanied by a little daughter, who rode a pretty pony with childish grace.

Newbern has become quite a jolly place to live in. It is filled with Yankee jimcracks, ranging all the way from top-boots to preserved strawberries. The market supplies splendid Northern apples, Southern ditto, cider, honey, ginger cakes, crackers, fish, preserved meats and fruits, oysters, pickles, condensed milk, chocolate, sugar, tea, coffee, military goods, &c. It is wonderfully convenient to be so near all these little comforts, *especially to those having a shot in the locker.*[13]

Gingerbread, pies, and even apple-dumplings, are brought to us by the negroes in profusion, while the sutlers furnish us with butter, cheese, sardines, and all the main essentials of luxurious living. Our regular rations are not to be sneezed at, although at present a scarcity of hops has thrown us back upon hard tack.[14] We are treated to beef steaks, excellent rice soups, fish, hash, &c.

The general health of the regiment continues good, although a few in each company are weakened by diarrhoea, and some few are yet suffering from colds and coughs contracted by our late exposures. The majority of the men, however, were never in better condition.

It is, perhaps, needless for me to inform you that the published report of the capture of a large rebel force near Plymouth, was a canard. I learn that the enterprising perpetrator of the story is under arrest.

Newspaper correspondents are not allowed to give all the news in this department, and any apparent deficiencies in my letters in the way of military intelligence can thus be easily accounted for. The Newbern Progress, I observe, omits to record the arrival of regiments, which would seem to be a very useless precaution, considering that the Boston and New York papers herald in advance the departure of every regiment for this department. I also notice that they are industriously posting up the rebels concerning a prospective expedition to Texas. A government that can afford to divulge its military plans in this way must be strong indeed.

We have received a copy of the New York Herald of the 15th inst., giving a brief account of our skirmish near Williamston. It is observed studiously to avoid giving the slightest credit to the 44th, which bore its full share of the brunt of the whole expedition, and acquitted itself in a manner to elicit the warm commendation of the General Commanding.

In my hurried account of our late march many incidents of the expedition were unavoidably omitted. All secesh men who might be useful to the enemy, resident along the road, were taken prisoners. Miserable looking fellows were they, as a rule, but quite handsome enough for their wives. In the house of one poor miserable paralytic wretch we found a double-barrelled gun, loaded and capped. "This is what picks off our men of nights," said a sergeant of cavalry, as he took possession of the shooter; and then, by a close examination, satisfied himself that the sick rebel was not playing possum. The scared and forlorn expression on the yellow and haggard face of his wife was a study for an artist.

As one decent looking farmer was taken from his house, an affectionate daughter followed the soldiers and besought them in shrieks of anguish to let her papa come back. Repeated assurances that her papa should not be hurt, seemed to afford her only very slight consolation.

Among our prisoners was a little curly-headed rebel sergeant who was taken captive at Roanoke Island and paroled. The contrabands in our train gave him the name of being a dreadfully severe master. He refused to take the oath, although once offering to do so at a time when he might have afforded his rebel friends valuable information of our strength and whereabouts. He managed his conversation with great shrewdness, and when, upon our return past his residence, he left us to go home, he no doubt chuckled over the information which he had artfully drawn from some of the garrulous fellows placed on guard over him.

Private [Cornelius C.] Lane, detailed as wagoner from Co. D, and who upon our march did yeoman's service as forager, claims the "first blood." He was searching a rebel's house for fire-arms, and being forcibly resisted in his efforts to secure one of these weapons, used the butt of a fowling piece over the head of secesh with such good effect that all resistance ceased.

The morning after our affair with the rebels at Chopper's Creek, or Rawles' Mill, as the place is variously called, a party of us went to a neighboring house to fill our canteens at the well. Three good looking women, a grey-haired mother and two daughters, sat in the piazza. The younger ones were handsome, and one was a widow in weeds.[15] The man of the house, a paralytic old gentleman, weighing three hundred and fifty pounds, sat in the centre of the hall running through the house. In the course of the artillery fire, the preceding night, a shot had passed through the floor of the piazza while the family were occupying it. The poor old man was too frightened to speak except in monosyllables. His wife besought us with streaming eyes to leave them alone—"they were only two poor old critters," although their son *had* been shooting at us from the woods a few hours before. The young woman in weeds, pale and pensive, said little. Her sister, who wouldn't acknowledge that she was frightened by the bombardment, boldly declared that she was a "seceder," and that "the meanest of all the critters was them as wouldn't stick up for their country." One of our soldiers courteously suggested that we were sticking up for the *whole* country, while she was only sticking up for a fraction of it. She replied that she was in favor of an undivided country so long as we could get along harmoniously, but when that became impossible, she became a "seceder." "We believe as our men say," she added, as a clincher.

At Williamston, in one of the deserted mansions, some of our boys fell upon an old piano, which, during our first few hours' tarry at that place, although mingling its notes with the voices of sacrificed pigs, resounded vigorously with old familiar airs, speaking eloquently of home and friends. The relic fever raged wildly at Williamston, and books, MSS. [manuscripts], and trinkets, some of considerable rarity and value, were carried away by our soldiers. The office of Judge [Asa] Biggs, an ex-U.S. Senator, contributed largely to allay the craving for spoils and relics which unfortunately possesses too many of our men.[16]

The last noticeable incident of the expedition was the arrest of the captain of the principal transport conveying our regiment. In coming down the Roanoke River with a schooner in tow, crowded with troops, the schooner was so unaccountably run ashore that the captain of the steamer was superseded by the mate and confined in his own cabin. After that we proceeded without much hindrance. The summary manner in which military authorities avail themselves of transports is doubtless not a little aggravating to the sovereigns of the quarter-deck, unaccustomed as they are to rivals near the throne.

As we read now-a-days of our poor fellows upon the Potomac shivering o' nights, for the want of overcoats and proper shelter, we sympathize with them most deeply, as our late experience has enabled us to do. It is difficult to exaggerate the discomfort of stretching one's self for sleep, without fire, upon wet ground, and that with wet, cold feet, growing colder and colder towards morning. On one occasion we were driven to our feet by rain, and on another by intense cold. We wonder that we endure these exposures, and not only live, but almost flourish under them. Our experience has already taught us something of the wonderful endurance and elasticity of the human frame, which rusts out through the enervation of idleness and vicious habits faster than it wears out by the sturdy hardships of the soldier.

We are again settling into barrack life and drill. Here is the daily order of performances:

Reveille, 6.30 A.M.; breakfast, 7; sergeant's report to adjutant, 7.15; surgeon's call, 7.30; guard mounting, 8; squad drills under sergeants, superintended by commissioned officers, 8.30 to 10; block drill for commissioned officers under lieut.-colonel, 10 to 11; company drill under lieutenants, 11 to 12; block drill for sergeants under captains, 11 to 12; dinner at 12; first sergeants' call, 1 P.M.; company drill, 1.30 to 2.30; battalion drill, 3 to 4; company parade, 4.30; dress parade, 5; supper, 6; tattoo, 7.30; taps, 8.30.

Among other items of regimental news is the commissioning of Charles C. Soule, formerly adjutant of the Fourth Battalion, as second lieutenant of the Newton company,[17] Captain [John A.] Griswold, in place of Lieutenant [Charles G.] Kendrick, promoted to the place made vacant by the resignation of First Lieutenant [Frank H.] Forbes. Lieutenant Soule had command of our camp in the absence of our regiment upon the expedition beyond Hamilton. He is now in Boston upon recruiting service, and any of our friends who may desire to make him the guardian of Thanksgiving or Christmas packages on their way hither, will take notice. We are already making arrangements for a Thanksgiving dinner as nearly like that New England institution as practicable.

We have named our camp "Stevenson," as a mark of esteem for the Colonel commanding our brigade. At the christening, three hearty cheers were given for him.

NOVEMBER 20, 1862.

It rains easily here in November, and to-day the windows of heaven are opened wide. We that should otherwise have been on drill, like it. The poor fellows on guard do not. The amount of letter-writing in this regiment is something astounding. Each mail carries from the 44th scarcely less than fifteen hundred missives to friends in Massachusetts. Pens and pencils are busy to-day. Some are darning their stockings, and have reason to bless the foresight which prepared those little bags of yarn, needles, &c., which they received at the hands of Mrs. Otis.

Thanksgiving Day, the 27th ult., was duly celebrated by the Massachusetts troops at this post. It would not have been observed with more feeling and *eclat* by the same individuals at home. It is to be questioned, even,
if the viands of a New England Thanksgiving, smoking upon the home
table, would have been eaten with so ardent a relish as that with which our
somewhat ruder dainties were devoured in barracks. My observations
were, of course, chiefly confined to our own regiment. Company F, as in
most other things, took the lead, and dined together as a company. Their
barracks and table presented a marvel of neatness and taste. The rough
walls were half obscured with holly branches and flags. The long table was
covered with a white cloth, crockery ware, and glass. Poultry, vegetables,
sauces, pies, puddings, cakes, roast beef, oysters, coffee and dessert helped
to make up their bill of fare; it was not found necessary to send beyond
Newbern for luxuries contrasting so pleasantly with "hard tack and salt
horse."[18] The dinner was gotten up by the rank and file, and private
[Francis C.] Hopkinson presided. A series of "regular toasts" were offered,
and the speeches which followed would have put to the blush the majority
of after-dinner efforts in "our Athens." The President of the United States
and the Old Commonwealth were fittingly eulogized, and the dear ones
at home were pathetically alluded to in song and speech. In the evening
Apollo and Terpsichore ruled the hour.[19]

In most of the other barracks the companies dined luxuriously. In a few
the company spirit proved insufficient to secure so much unanimity; but
there were numerous cheerful messes, ample spreads, and afterwards a due
amount of colic. Companies G,E,H,C,D and A. and perhaps others, got
up evening dances or literary entertainments. The day was made a complete holiday, all drill, and even dress parade, being omitted. The Massachusetts 5th, and some other regiments and companies, indulged in mock
dress parades, which produced very sidesplitting effects indeed. The act-

ing Major of the Fifth appeared in a complete undress uniform of red flannel, most of the men with their garments inside out, and wearing haversacks upon their heads. There were several fine personations of Falstaff, and one man in armor, to wit, an army stove, through the door of which he made his observations. The manual presented some amusing varieties of the Hardee, and the first sergeants were ordered "to their posts-quick!"[20] Altogether the Fifth are said to have equalled the best exhibition of the Antiques and Horribles.[21] Among the spectators was [military] Governor [Edward] Stanley [Stanly].

So passed Thanksgiving in the country of the enemy. We could not have asked for a jollier one, but God grant that the next may be in New England, and for new and more powerful reasons than has yet impelled us to perpetuate the example of the Pilgrims.

At dress parade Friday evening, Colonel Lee complimented the regiment for its appropriate observance of the previous day, and for the good order before and after taps.

As respects future military movements in the department, your correspondent is mum. We have but a few sick, and the few wounded are doing well.

We have organized a regimental choir under Charley Ewer, of Company D. Drum-Major [George L.] Babcock has got his corps in good working order, and is now laboring industriously in organizing a band. We have the loan of a set of instruments, but they may be called for at an early day; so our friends in Boston may now gratify themselves in their long-cherished scheme of presenting us a set of instruments.

The Massachusetts 8th, Colonel [F. J.] Coffin, and the 51st, Colonel [Augustus B. R.] Sprague, arrived at Newbern last evening. We have the happiness of treating them to hot coffee.

I need scarcely remind the friends at home how anxiously we shall look for "boxes" between this and Christmas. The latest arrived transports were supposed to bring a great number of those interesting articles, and to-night a numerous squad was despatched to the town to bring them to camp. There proved to be about one box to each two hundred men. I will just mention that we have not seen the paymaster.

This letter and many others will be taken to Boston by Rev. Charles F. Barnard, whose familiar form appeared to us this evening at dress parade. He officiated at the evening services, and made some stirring remarks to the regiment. Mr. Barnard has one son in the 44th and another in the 24th.

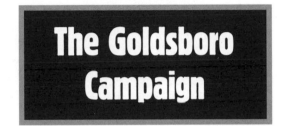

CHAPTER 5

The Goldsboro Campaign

Newbern, N.C.,

DEC. 22, 1862.

A correspondent who marches with rifle and knapsack will not be expected to compete with the cavaliers of the New York press, whose business it is to glean facts and send them forward by the earliest and swiftest messengers. You will have heard that we have been on another expedition, the prominent results of which were three successful engagements with the enemy, and the destruction of a large railroad bridge on the road connecting Goldsboro' with Warrington [Wilmington]. We marched one hundred and fifty miles in ten days, and came back to Newbern in a more dilapidated condition than after our trip to the vicinity of Tarboro'.[1] The expedition included four brigades under General [Henry W.] Wessells, lately stationed near Suffolk, Virginia, Colonel [Thomas G.] Stevenson, Colonel [Thomas J. C.] Amory, and Colonel [Horace C.] Lee, of the

27th. The regiments were the Massachusetts 3d, 5th, 17th, 23d, 24th, 25th, 43d, 44th, 45th, 46th, and 51st; the New York 85th, 92d, and 96th; the Pennsylvania 85th, 101st, and 103d; New Jersey 9th; Connecticut 10th, and Rhode Island 5th. Besides these was a considerable force of cavalry and nearly fifty pieces of artillery, including Belger's Rhode Island and the New York 3d artillery. Altogether our force could not have fallen much below fifteen thousand men.[2]

Our first two days' march up the Trent road [toward Kinston] was not marred by any extraordinary adventures. We were in heavy marching order, and experienced terrible fatigue. Straggling commenced the first day, and was kept up until our return. On the second day our progress was slightly impeded by trees felled across the road, the burning of a bridge, and a skirmish with the enemy's pickets, in which we killed some and took some prisoners. We saw one dead rebel stretched upon a piazza as we passed a house on our right, and marvelled at the stolid indifference of two or three white women who sat near the corpse and gazed at us as though nothing unusual had happened. At one point the column was confronted by a spunky secesh female, who, with a heavy wooden rake, stood guard over her winter's store of sweet potatoes. Her eye flashed defiance, but so long as she stood upon the defensive no molestation was offered her. When, however, she concluded to change her tactics, and slapped a cavalry officer in the face, gone were her sweet potatoes and other stores in the twinkling of an eye.

On Sunday, our fourth day from Newbern, we were drawn up in line of battle about one mile from Kinston, a large rebel town on the Neuse.[3] The duty of the right wing of the 44th was to deploy as skirmishers and pass through a swamp to the right of the road, which was defended by a strong rebel battery near the river. We were *led* forward by Colonel Lee. As we approached the swamp, we met the wounded of the Massachusetts 45th and Connecticut 10th, who had preceded us. It was not a very reassuring spectacle, and we plunged knee deep into the mud and peat before us, under the firm expectation that bloody work awaited us as well as our predecessors. In this, however, we were happily disappointed. We found the swamp strewed with blankets and soldiers' gearing, and just upon the further outskirts of the place lay a number of the dead of the 45th. As we emerged into the opening beyond we expected to confront a force of rebel infantry, but were again agreeably disappointed. The first rebels we saw was a long file of rebel prisoners which were just then passing by us on our left. Advancing a few rods further to join our left wing, which had gone forward by the road, we had scarcely got in sight of our artillery before another squad of rebel soldiers issued from the wood between our guns and the river, with a flag of truce and delivered themselves up.

We soon knew by the cheers that went up that the day was ours. How it was achieved we did not exactly know then, but we heard of brave and gallant deeds by the Connecticut 10th, the New Jersey 9th and the Peninsula soldiers.[4] You will have seen by the lists of killed and wounded that there was hard fighting, and that the rebels made a determined stand. After the smoke of battle had cleared away, we found ourselves in possession of a rebel battery and about five hundred prisoners. We found that we had possession of the bridge crossing the river to Kinston, the rebels having been forced to beat such a hasty retreat as not to have time to fire the structure. One man in attempting the operation by the aid of spirits of turpentine, burned himself to death. The rebels left loaded guns near the fire which they kindled, and one of them put an end to the life of Col. Gray of the New York 96th, who was assisting his men to extinguish the flames.

The scene of the conflict was the most beautiful which we have yet witnessed in North Carolina. It was an elevated field on the southerly shore of the Neuse, whose course is here marked by a fringe of fine trees through which the white buildings and spires of Kinston were observable a mile distant. The mangled condition of the trees and shrubbery near the road, or wherever the artillery or infantry guns ranged, gave proof of extremely hot work. Major [John G.] Chambers, who commanded the 23d, said ten thousand rebel bullets whistled over the head of his regiment while it supported one of our batteries.

It is said that the enemy had a force of seven regiments under the command of Gen. [Nathan G.] Evans, of South Carolina.[5] The men we took as prisoners were of the rawest and most miserable description. Some of them had been hurried down from Raleigh that morning. They regarded their captivity with great equanimity, not to say cheerfulness. They were doubtless all paroled. Among them were several field and line officers.

Sunday night we passed in Kinston, bivouacing on the borders of the town. As we passed through the streets upon our first entrance we found many bales of cotton piled up and set on fire. The Kinston rebels no doubt thought we were dying to get possession of their precious staple. Near the depot a great pile of corn was also on fire, and afforded a splendid bivouac blaze for some of our troops. A few Union people we found here. One lady hospitably entertained some of the officers, and afforded interesting information of the enemy's hopes and discomfiture. They confidently expected to hold the place, but left with great precipitancy, strewing the way with clothing, equipments, guns, &c.

The next day (Monday) we recrossed the river and proceeded towards Goldsboro'. Tuesday noon we reached Whitehall bridge, which, however, had been burned by the rebels, who were there in force to dispute our passage. As usual they were all under cover, with riflemen securely posted near the opposite bank. The ball opened with the thunder of artillery on both sides. At the same time several brigades of our infantry were hurried forward and deployed on either side [of] the road to reply to the volleys of the sharpshooters in ambuscade. Our regiment was posted on the edge of a hill near the river, directly behind a Virginia rail-fence. Here we lay down and loaded and fired across the river, until we began to find ourselves the objects of particular attention. Eight of our men were killed or mortally wounded, and fourteen others less seriously injured. Of the killed, two men in Co. A were struck down by a solid shot, while we were hurrying forward to the post assigned us.

Our place soon became so warm that Belger's battery of artillery was sent to our relief, when we fell back and supported it while it shelled the opposite shore. But the sharpshooters were too securely posted to be disturbed, and commenced picking off our horses, greatly to the disgust of Capt. [James] Belger, who soon ascertained that he was throwing his shot away. In the meantime the rebel artillery had been silenced, and the column soon resumed its march up the southerly side of the river. During the engagement at Whitehall, a company of sharpshooters was hastily organized, and it is believed that some of the rebels got a Roland for their Oliver.[6] "Old Stars," of Co. D, who is equally familiar with shooting stars and shooting sticks, is confident of bringing down a man.[7] Col. Lee and Major [Charles W.] Dabney, both experienced riflemen, took part with the sharpshooters, and were also noticed to present somewhat too conspicuous marks for the riflemen on the other side. The daring of all our field officers and chaplain has been established beyond question. None of the rest of the regiment have been so much exposed as they.

Beside destroying the bridge at Whitehall, the rebels destroyed two gunboats constructing at that point, and thereby saved us the trouble of the operation.

The following is a complete list of the killed and wounded at the battle of Whitehall:[8]

Co. A. Killed—Albert L. Butler, D. Tyler Newcomb, J. Mason Slocumb, M. R. Meagher. Wounded—A. H. Everett, A. S. May, J. F. Berry, Sergt. J. F. Clark, A. K. Tappan, J. W. Greenwood, Wm. Bamford.

Co. B. Wounded (accidental)—A. H. Everett.

Co. C. Killed—Sergt. A. Stacy Courtis, Corp. E. H. Curtis, Antonio F. Pollo.

Co. K. Killed—Geo. E. Noyes.

Co. D. Wounded—Charles C. Ewer, Frederic Jackson.

Co. F. Wounded—J. F. Dean.

Co. G. Wounded—Francis E. Lincoln, E. S. Fisher.

Co. H. Wounded—Sergt. [William W.] Howe, E. C. Crosby.

George H. Colby, of Company D, detailed for duty on the signal corps, was seriously wounded in one of his arms while going up the river Neuse, with his party, to act in concert with the expedition. Their boat was fired at a number of times, and several rebel batteries were subsequently cleaned out by our gunboats, which now go up within a short distance of Kinston, where they met our returning column with a supply of provisions.

A few miles beyond Whitehall we bivouaced for the night, and the next day pressed on to Everettsville, a short distance from Golbsboro', where we had the happiness of destroying a long tressel-work bridge on the railroad connecting Goldsborough with Wilmington. Here again we met the enemy in force, but as our regiment was held in reserve, I have only a hearsay statement of the incidents of the fight. The cannonading was long and fierce, and the rebels made a dash to capture one of our batteries, but were repulsed with very serious slaughter. I hear they attempted the flag of truce dodge once too often. Whether or not it was the intention of General Foster to push on to Goldsborough, it became apparent at this point that we could safely advance no farther, owing to the scarcity of our provisions and artillery ammunition, so we turned about and went back to Newbern, where our advance arrived last Saturday night.

The expedition was favored with extraordinarily fine weather; but even under this most favorable circumstance, the march was one of unusual severity. Some of the Peninsular soldiers said it outdid their previous experience, and that they never before witnessed so much straggling. We bivouaced every night without shelter, but were kept tolerably comfortable by our rubber and woollen blankets.

The assembled bivouac fires of fifteen thousand men present a spectacle of rare beauty. I notice that a recent number of Leslie's Illustrated contains a graphic and truthful picture of "Going into Camp." The rail gathering is to the life. You can imagine how much we are indebted to the rail fences of Secessia. They give us comfortable fires, hot coffee, and sometimes shelter itself. I can hardly conceive how we could live without them. Perhaps we are equally indebted to the pigs and potatoes of the country, for soldiers certainly never could march ten days upon hard tack and coffee alone. Upon leaving the barracks each man is provided with a little bag of coffee and sugar mixed; so he always has at hand the means for a comforting and strengthening draught. This is found extremely convenient in the many cases where the cooks and wagons fail to come [in] time by reason of break-downs or other delays on the road.

I have spoken of stragglers upon the march. There are two or three distinct kinds of straggling. One is involuntary—the result of sickness or exhaustion. Another comes from laziness or the want of a spirited determination to bear up; and another from cowardice. Do not imagine that because a man enlists and goes to the wars that he necessarily does his whole duty as a soldier. There are no better opportunities for shirking than those afforded the soldier. It was noticeable upon our late march that whenever cannonading commenced at the head of the column, as it did day after day, scores of men commenced falling out and laying down by the side of the road. This was peculiarly the case with some of the old regiments, and I think there were few of the new ones but exhibited their cowards and sneaks on these occasions in this way.

I am now obliged to close this hurried and meagre account, asking the reader to remember that among the really "played out" soldiers of the late expedition is "Corporal."

P.S. I am authorized to thank numerous friends for many Christmas boxes. God bless the thoughtful friends at home.

CHAPTER 6

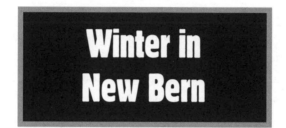

Winter in
New Bern

Newbern, N.C.,

JAN. 2, 1863.

The proprietor of the Herald has the warm thanks of the 44th regiment for a kind remembrance in the shape of a generous bundle of Sunday Heralds, evidently made up without regard to the increased price of paper. I believe it is the pretty general opinion of our boys that no paper quite so well meets the requirements of Massachusetts soldiers as the Sunday Herald,—a fact which our great constituency of friends in Boston appears to appreciate. Its department of military news is the most complete given by any Boston paper; and the same may be said of its musical and dramatic columns, to which our theatre-loving and theatre-hungry boys turn with an ever sharpening appetite. The spice and point of its editorial articles are not less admired. So much by way of encouragement to the hard-working fellows at No. 6 Williams Court.

Since our return from Goldsboro', a little more than a week ago, we have been considerately respited from drill and work generally. A ten days' tension of our utmost physical power left us in a very "chawed up" condition, independent of the colds contracted and the feet made sore; and we stood in good need of the week's rest which has been granted us. I am wondering if the troops in this department are an exception to the general rule, and if newspaper correspondents really tell the truth when they assert the anxiety of the soldiers of the Potomac and elsewhere for advances, forward movements, &c. &c. I have yet to be introduced to the soldier who desires a repetition of these little excursions of Gen. Foster, and who wouldn't give his nine months' pay and bounty for the certainty of serving his country as well by remaining at Newburn [sic] during the rest of his term of service. At the same time, I do not know but that we are as brave and patriotic as the average. Let me assure you, dear friends at home, that none beside the soldier can fully apprehend the full tests of patriotism, or the difference between preaching and practice as applied to love of country.

The soldier who unmurmuringly meets and performs his duties of hardship and danger must be provided with something of that divine armor which fits him to be a soldier of the cross. The man who says he loves to face the "leaden rain and iron hail" of battle is either a liar or a monstrosity. No man who cares for life and friends can go into battle without a natural shudder and dread. The wonder is that duty and pride are strong enough in any man to urge him forward into the very teeth of death. Let us be [as] charitable as possible toward the white-livered wretches who fall out of the ranks at the first bidding of the cannon's voice.

Among the severely wounded at Whitehall was Charley Ewer, the regimental chorister. The sweetness of his voice was the type of a character which had endeared him greatly to his comrades. He was shot through one of the lungs, and his condition is most critical. The places he made musical are now dumb and sad. We hope a deeper gloom may not settle on them.

Our new band is making rather wonderful progress. They are a jolly set of fellows, the band, with no marching, no fighting, no drilling, no guarding to do. Hardly an even thing, perhaps; but, then, the band is a great ornament at inspections and dress parades, and we can't help feeling some pride in it.

Since the holidays commenced the friends of the men in the regiment have overwhelmed us with the bounties and luxuries of home. Here are the contents of one box that came under the especial observation of your correspondent, and which he regards as a model in its way: tea, coffee, sugar, butter, pepper, salt, capsicum, cheese, gingerbread, confectioner's cakes, bologna sausage, condensed milk, smoked halibut, pepper-box, camp knife, matches, ink, mince pie, candy, tomato ketchup, apples, horse radish, emery paper, sardines, cigars, smoking tobacco, candles, soap, newspapers, pictorials, letters, pickles, and *cholera mixture*. The opening of this box, and the examination and display of its contents, furnished an evening of rare enjoyment. The arrival and distribution of these boxes at the Quartermaster's are attended by some very animated scenes. I am sorry to say that Mr. Sutler Grant's schooner is detained in the stream by red tape. He has a number of boxes for us.

Christmas was less extensively observed than Thanksgiving at Newbern, although not a few of us were enabled to indulge in a dinner a little better than usual. One or two of the barracks were trimmed with evergreen, and something like amusement was attempted by the aid of contraband minstrelsy [minstrels] and dancers.

Last night, New Year's, we were favored with the

SECOND

DRAMATIC AND MUSICAL ENTERTAINMENT

BY THE

44TH REGIMENTAL DRAMATIC ASSOCIATION.

Prologue (original)	Henry T. Reed.
Overture	Band.
Recitation (selected)	F. D. Wheeler.
Song	Quartette Club.

| Recitation | C. A. Chase. |
| Recitation (humorous) | E. L. Hill. |

BAND.

After which the Grand Trial Scene from

THE MERCHANT OF VENICE.

Shylock	H. T. Reed.
Duke	W. Howard.
Antonio	D. F. Safford.
Bassanio	F. D. Wheeler.
Gratiano	J. H. Waterman.
Portia	L. Miller.
Solanio	F. A. Sayers.

BAND.

Followed by

A GRAND MINSTREL SCENE.

Opening Chorus	Company.
Louisiana Lowlands	H. Howard.
Dolly Day	F. A. Sayers.
Shells of the Ocean	H. Howard.
Susianna Simpkins	F. A. Sayers.
Ham Fat Man	J. H. Myers.

Concluding with

A TERRIBLE CAT-ASS-TROPHE

ON THE NORTH ATLANTIC RAILROAD.

Characters by the Company.

Director	H. T. Reed.
Assistant Manager	D. F. Safford.
Secretary	W. Howard.
Treasurer	J. M. Waterman.

Executive Committee: F. D. Wheeler, L. Miller, F. A. Sayers.

The order of exercises was [given] upon neatly-printed handbills.

Since the Federal occupation of Kinston, work upon the railroad from Newbern to the former town has been vigorously prosecuted; but recently the rebels have taken a characteristic fancy to drive in our workmen and rip up their work.

The troops in North Carolina have been constituted an army corps, of which several division are to be formed in due time. Brigadier-General [Henry W.] Wessells has already been assigned to command a division. Col. [Thomas G.] Stevenson has received his stars, and his brigade will be the second of Wessells's division, the first being composed of the Pennsylvania and New York troops, lately under his command as brigadier, and now under Gen. [Lewis Cass] Hunt, from the Potomac army. The other divisions will probably be commanded by some of the new Brigadiers in this department, of whom one is Gen. [Charles A.] Hickman, lately Colonel of the New Jersey 9th. Gen. Stevenson's brigade comprises the Mass. 8th, 24th, and 44th, the Rhode Island 5th, and the Conn. 10th. The 44th will be the only new regiment in Gen. Wessells's division.[1]

We are glad our friends at the North derive so much satisfaction and encouragement from our late raid up the valley of the Neuse. Since our return, it has formed a subject of lively contemplation among those engaged in it. I notice by the rebel papers that secesh was well apprised of two facts about us, to wit: that we were short of artillery ammunition, and also of provision. It occurred to your correspondent that the cannoniers were quite too communicative of the first fact. The blabbing of soldiers is really one of the greatest of nuisances, not to say curses, connected with our army. Supposed facts and conjectures are retailed by them with never slacking industry, and with equal assurance and recklessness, a hear-say or rumor immediately taking rank with truth itself in the minds and mouths of a miserable set of *quid nuncs* [gossipers] which infest every company of every regiment.

As to our being out of provisions, our systematic and extensive foraging was the best proof of the low condition of our hard tack and salt horse. There were days when we got very hungry indeed, when visions of past luxuries haunted the mind like torturing ghosts. Baked beans chiefly afflicted the soul of your correspondent. They would not down at his bidding. Neither would that little coffee-pot on the warm range at midnight, where it was wont to stand when I came home from the labor of the newspaper sanctum. We found way-side turnip patches sources of great relief and substantial refreshment, but our chief subsistence was the pigs, cattle, and sweet potatoes of the country. With a little lard, a little corn meal, and sweet potatoes sliced and fried, we were soon enabled to forget a day's fatigue. Poultry and slices of tenderloin sometimes fell to the lot of a few who supped royally.

During the fight at Everettsville [near Goldsboro] the soldiers of the reserve busied themselves with eating turnips and gazing at the conflict. In the midst of the cannonade, a lively charge was made by our brigade on a mound of sweet potatoes between us and the enemy. Subsequently, at night, while we deployed in the woods in anticipation of a pursuit of our retiring column, we consoled ourselves by munching the sweet potatoes we had stowed in our pockets and haversacks.

That night's countermarching is never to be forgotten for its wild and picturesque beauty. Fires were running on either side of the road. The ground was spread with a carpet of flame, and the resinous pine were as pillars of fire. The beautiful scenes thus afforded cheered our march wonderfully, and engraved pictures on the mind which will endure as long as memory.

Among other items of regimental news I will mention the resignation of Captain Reynolds, on account of ill health. Captain Lombard is much reduced by illness, and will probably resign,—in which event the regiment will lose one of its best and bravest officers. Capt. Lombard and his first lieutenant Geo. Lombard both distinguished themselves for pluck and coolness at the midnight skirmish near Williamston.

Newbern, N.C.,

The uncertainty of the mails to and from this place, and the unaccountable delay in the publication of some of my letters, are the causes which have operated to prevent my writing with the frequency of a few weeks ago. If I could say it without appearance of egotism, I should like to observe that few correspondents beside "Corporal" can have stronger incentives to continue his communications, if he might judge by the reception which the friends of the 44th have given his letters thus far, and the acknowledgements which it has been his pleasure to receive. So much in return.

My stock of regimental gossip is not abundant this time. Since my last we have been visited by the paymaster. How it happens that nine months' regiments, and bounty regiments at that, are paid off, while old regiments, which have not seen the paymaster for six or nine months, are skipped, passeth the understanding of even the favored ones like ourselves. It is a circumstance certainly not calculated to improve the relations between the old and new regiments, none the best at present.

Since the advent of the paymaster, we have had a less agreeable camp visitor in the shape of malarious fever. Several deaths from this complaint have already occurred, and a number of dangerous cases are in the hospital. The malady attacks with great suddenness, and is attended with much delirium and distress. As a measure of prevention the regiment is served with quinine every evening.

Many of the regiments are renewedly cheered and made grateful by the reception of home comforts. Your correspondent must be pardoned for laying some stress on this pleasant feature of our experience. The delayed schooners of Sutler Grant have at last arrived with their precious freights. Time, it is to be confessed, had made its mark upon some of the poultry and pastry, but that which had been sealed in tin cans or boxes arrived in fine condition, although nearly a month in transit. As friends express themselves in much doubt as to what is best to send, here are the contents of a box recently received, which may be taken as a model: A large sealed tin of mince pies and cake; a large sealed tin box of cake; a large paper box of ditto [cake]; a tin box of sugar; a tin box of pepper; a jar of pickles; a box of eggs; together with apples, pears, pens, stationery, and last but not least, letters. A portion of one of the latter articles I subjoin [append]. It may also be regarded as a model:

There are so many articles we wish to send you, but so few which we feel sure will reach you unspoiled, that it has required considerable thought and discussion on our part, in regard to the particular articles which shall be sent. But if you take one half the pleasure in receiving and consuming them that it has given us to prepare them, we shall be more than happy.

I hope the vessel which carries out this little box may go freighted with many good things prepared by loving hearts and willing hands to give comfort to the soldiers.

The most that I can do for you and the brave men who have so cheerfully and nobly gone forth to put down this wicked rebellion, seems so little, when compared with the sacrifices you have made, that it seems hardly worth thinking of; and yet, when we send off our loved ones to this terrible war, we feel the sacrifices are not all on your side.

I have a dear young brother in Banks's Expedition,[2] who has gone to lay down his young life, if needed; and hard as it was to give him up, I feel more proud of him than I ever did before.

Another thing we have to wonder about, and that is, whether you may not be in want of some stockings. Those long wearisome marches you have made must wear out shoes and stockings as well as feet.

Now, be it known unto you, it is no trouble to do what we can for the soldier, particularly when that soldier is a friend. It would give us untold pleasure to supply you with some of those very useful articles, if you will let your wants be known.

"Corporal" and other innocent persons have lately experienced the novel sensation of a night drill, as an atonement for the sins of a few young gentlemen addicted to throwing hard bread about the barracks, and charging pipes and candles with gunpowder. This species of vicarous punishment, in which officers and privates are alike involved, is one of the odd peculiarities of military justice to which we sometimes have to submit with the best grace possible under the circumstances.

The favor of our friends at home is bespoken in behalf of a memorial volume of the 44th Regiment soon to be put in press under the editorship of Mr. [De Forest] Safford, of Company F.[3] Its contents will be furnished by the members of the regiment, and will have exclusive reference to its history.

Whatever it may lack in completeness and finish will be easily attributable to the circumstances attending the compilation of the work, the editor and contributors being working soldiers.

We are in the occasional receipt from Boston of third-hand private reports reflecting upon the bravery of our regiment upon various occasions; and now, coupled with one of these slanders, comes a story charging Quartermaster [Francis] Bush with gross and contemptible frauds upon the men, such as stealing their boxes, blankets and other articles sent by friends at the North. The last story, absurd as it is, is as true as the first, and both, I hardly need say, are malicious falsehoods—the one class of reports being systematically manufactured and circulated by men in one or two of the old regiments from Massachusetts, who will never forgive us because we were voted bounties *after* we had enlisted.

Since writing the above my attention has been called to a paragraph in a letter "from the 27th and 46th Regiments," in which the 44th Regiment is accused of refusing to charge at the battle of Kinston. The accusation is wholly and unqualifiedly false. The 44th did all it was told to do at Kinston, and it was personally complimented for its behavior by General Foster, as we marched by him into town. I confess that I undertake to reply to these slanders with very little patience. The individual who was induced to send them north for publication showed less sagacity than the reporter of the New York Herald, who was actually approached with a bribe to make certain statements derogatory to the 44th, and touching points of which he could have no personal knowledge. I have this from the Herald reporter's own mouth; and the reader will judge how far it goes to confirm the suspicion of a systematic purpose to do us an injury.

Lieutenant [Richard H.] Weld has been elected Captain of Company K, in place of Captain [Frank W.] Reynolds, resigned; and Second Lieutenant [Fred T.] Brown, who becomes First Lieutenant, is succeeded by Sergeant [John] Parkinson. Lieutenant George H. Lombard succeeds to the captaincy of Company C, by the resignation of Captain Jacob H. Lombard, and Sergeant [William] Hedge becomes First Lieutenant. Lieutenant [James W.] Briggs, of this company, is serving on the signal corps.

The names of those who have recently died in camp, of malarious fever, are [John C.] Pollitz and [Joshua] Moody, of Company F; [Henry G.] Kimball, of Company G; and [Alfred B.] Moulton, of Company C. The prevalence of this disease is attributed to the dryness of the season. It is not confined to one regiment. When the swamps which surround us are filled with rain, the cause will be removed.

At dress parade last evening the following order was read:

> In consideration of and as a reward for their brave deeds at Kinston, Whitehall and Goldsborough, the Commanding General directs that the regiments and batteries which accompanied the expedition to Goldsborough inscribe upon their banners these victories:
>
> Kinston, December 14th, 1862.
> Whitehall, December 16th, 1862.
> Goldsborough, December 17th, 1862.
>
> The Commanding General hopes that all future fields will be so fought that the record of them may be kept by inscription on the banners of the regiments engaged.

Newbern, N.C.,

JAN. 23, 1863.

The first grand Terpsichorean festival of the New Year in our regiment transpired on the evening of the 20th instant, in the barracks of Co. D. The much lamented absence of the feminine element was in part atoned for by female apparel donned for the occasion by a number of young men with smooth faces and an eye to artistic effect. If Jenkins[4] had been present his pencil would have waxed eloquent over the superb attire and tasteful colors of the magnificent blonde, Miss C. D. N. His page would have glowed with lover-like panegyrics of the tall and peerless, white-robed queen of the night, Miss G. F. B. Good taste, however, might have suggested that the former was a little too *en bon point* [plump], as well as too demonstrative in her personal decorations, and that the latter was a trifle tall for the breadth of her raiment. But when Jenkins came to the Misses C. F. W., J. H. W., W. G. R. and especially to Miss C. W. S., of East Boston, he would assuredly have "slopped over" in his characteristic manner. Not, however, because these Hebes were less faulty in toilet than the others, for a critical eye might have suggested dresses higher in the neck, longer in skirt, and less protuberant in the rear; less suggestive, in short, of those gay and festive occasions which have rendered Joe Clash and North street immortal the world over.[5] Some of the gallants of the young women were scarcely less stunning in their make up. The insignia of military office, from that of Major Generals to Lieutenants, extensively prevailed. Dancing, of course, was the order of the night; a fiddler was engaged, and

When music arose with its voluptuous swell,

Soft eyes looked love to eyes which spake again,

And all went merry as a marriage bell.

The following is the

ORDER OF DANCES.

1. Sicilian Circle,	March to Tarboro'.
2. Quadrille,	New England Guards.
3. Polka Quadrille,	Kinston Gallop.
4. Quadrille,	Yankee Doodle.

INTERMISSION.

Waltz, Polka Redowa, Schottische.

5. Quadrille,	Bloody 44th Quickstep.
6. Les Lanciers,	Connecticut 10th March.
7. Quadrille,	Lee's March.
8. Contra (Virginia Reel),	Rebels' Last Skedaddle.

In this connection I will introduce the managerial card, which was as follows:

GRAND BALL.

Sir:—The pleasure of your company, with ladies, is respectfully solicited at a Grand Ball, to be held in the Grand Parlor of the FIFTH AVENUE HOTEL, (No. 4 Newbern,) on TUESDAY EVENING, January 20th, 1863.

The Management beg leave to state that nothing will be left undone on their part to make it the party of the season.

MANAGERS.

C. H. Demeritt,   W. Howard,   J. E. Leighton.

COMMITTEE OF ARRANGEMENTS.

Benj. F. Burchsted, C. D. Newell, W. G. Reed, H. D. Stanwood
W. E. Savery, F. A. Sayer, F. M. Flanders, H. Howard
J. B. Gardner, Joe Simonds, Charles Adams, G. W. Hight.

MUSIC.

Quintzelbottom's Grand Quadrille and Serenade Band.
(One Violin.)

TICKETS $00.03 EACH, TO BE HAD OF THE MANAGERS.

No Postage Stamps or Sutler's Checks taken in payment.
N.B. Ladies will be allowed to smoke.
Persons wishing carriages will please apply to LIEUT. WHITE,
of the Ambulance Corps.
Persons wishing anything stronger than Water are referred
to the "Sanitary."[6]

The managers were decorated with official rosettes, a solid square of hard tack forming the centre of each. Even some of the belles of the evening were resplendent with pendant jewels cut from the same tenacious mineral.

That nothing might be wanting to revive the memories of Clash's Hall, a bar was improvised inside the sliding door where we get out rations, and here the cooks busily regaled the dancers with water, and molasses and water, from a bottle and a single tumbler, while announcing, by means of placards over the window, "Splendid New Drinks," in the shape of quinine and diarrhoea mixture No. 3, names forever associated with the articulate in the surgeon's matutinal bugle-call.[7] The bar soon began to show its effects in the shape of cocked hats, awry toilets, loud-mouthed controversies, and, at last, fighting. The intervention of an active but diminutive policeman was invoked. He was a little man, but chewed tobacco with a serious determination, which boded danger to evil doers. His services in keeping back the crowd and quelling disturbances in the vicinity of the bar were in constant requisition. Not unfrequently his badge was seen tossing in the midst of a riotous crowd, and he was reported to be once seen skedaddling before a slightly superior force. He was noticed as being very familiar with your reporter, whom he furnished with considerable doubtful information about his own operations.

Federal soldiers at New Bern, North Carolina, 1863. Courtesy of the Southern Historical Collection, University of North Carolina at Chapel Hill (Herman Biggs Papers).

At the proper hour refreshments were served. "A beautiful slave," in the person of Mr. West Williams, heretofore mentioned in these letters, entered with two trays containing severally hard tack and salt horse.[8] His advent was hailed with the same shouts and swaying of the crowd as usually attend the administration of our rations. The tack and horse vanished, and the dance proceeded with various divertisements [*sic*] to the end.

We had many visitors, including Colonel Lee and staff, all of whom evinced their intense satisfaction with what they heard and saw.

It is expected that other balls, including a masquerade, will succeed this affair.

A soldier's life is one of curious contrasts. Although not always gay, it has the jolliest kind of episodes. It affords the two emotional extremes. One day finds him in the midst of hilarity and social enjoyment, the next in the blood and carnage of battle, with friends falling all about him

"Thick as autumnal leaves in Valambrosa."

But an hour or two before the festivities recounted above, a slow-moving procession with muffled drum and reversed arms, moved from our lines with the remains of a much-loved comrade suddenly stricken down with the malarious fever. His name was [George F.] Boynton, of Company G. A day or two previously, Corporal [Adfur J.] Upham of the same company died of the same disease.

Newbern, N.C.,

JAN. 27, 1863.

The prevalence of malarious fever among some of the soldiers in this department at this season has created a little excitement, and I hope no exaggerated stories concerning it will reach the ears of our friends at the North. Since my last but two fatal cases have occurred, making eight in all. The last two deceased were [Walter S.] Bradbury of Co. C, and [William F.] Ingraham of Co. F.

Malarious fever, although characteristic of this locality in summer, was not anticipated here after the early frosts; but the succeeding severe drouth so reduced the bulk of water in the neighboring swamps as to leave a margin of mud, which has sent forth the fever poison. It is not sure, however, that our miserably contracted barracks have nothing to do with this disease.

While by the army regulations of England and France, each soldier in barracks is allowed a thousand cubic feet of air and space, we are allowed but two hundred and fifty in which to live and move and have our being; in which to eat and sleep, and read and write, and to store our effects. English and French barracks, generous as they are in space, are still provided with a commissary room in which to store any private ration which the men may fortunately possess; but American soldiers must make bunk-fellows of their butter, pies and pickles, or go without them. Then again, our barracks at Newbern are constructed of wet, unseasoned lumber, fresh from unhealthy swamps, so that upon the walls and roof of some of them, green mould gathers. All these circumstances are at least suggestive of something; if they are not, what's the matter? There are certainly no reasons why American barracks should not be the largest and best in the world.

We are surely not deficient in space, materials, or in constructive ingenuity, among the soldiers who are detailed to build and fit up quarters. No sane man would herd cattle together so closely as we are herded, for fear of breeding distemper. They are well-settled facts that soldiers upon the march, and bivouacing every night in the open air, are in better health than when living in barracks; and that marching and bivouacing cure the colds contracted by means of frequent sudden changes from close barracks to the open air.

In my last I gave you some account of an extemporized ball in the barrack of Co. D. Since then a grand masquerade has been held under the auspices of Co. E, our nearest left hand neighbor. Only a few hours were given to preparation, but the affair assumed an extent, as well as an appearance of elegance and grotesque humor not a little surprising, considering the limited resources of soldiers in camp. The members of the regiment were forewarned of the entertainment by the following notice:

BAL MASQUE.

A Grand Regimental *Bal Masque* will be held to-night, Jan. 24th, at the barrack of Co. E. None admitted except commissioned officers and those *en costume.*

The restriction was of little avail. Those who failed to pass the door keepers entered at the ventilators, and there was soon assembled the largest audience of the season. There were many masked and assumed characters, but the favorite and prevailing assumption was that of a girl. This was uniformly excellent, showing beyond doubt a close and enthusiastic devotion to the study of the character in the original. If you may trust the taste of your Jenkins, Miss K., of Co. F, was the belle of the occasion, although our public opinion is divided between that lady and Miss A., of Co. G, Miss R., of Co. E, the Misses H. and the Misses S., of Co. D, Miss H., of Co. A, and some others. I regret the poverty of vocabulary that prevents my describing their costumes. All of them were tasteful and some elegant. One lady of color attracted a large share of attention.[9] Several personations of the Prince of Darkness were voted admirable. Not the worst Satan was a young divinity student of Co. D, who had evidently studied his role. Bird o' Freedom [George W.] Sawin was there as a Pilgrim Father. There were harlequins, clowns, policemen, men of impenetrable visage, and one venerable monk with crucifix and beads. The barrack was brilliantly lighted by the aid of chandeliers, and there were, of course, music and dancing. Nearly all our officers were present, including the field and staff, together with several officers and privates from our excellent neighbor, the gallant Connecticut 10th, endeared to us alike by their signal bravery in the field of battle, and their cordial friendship toward us as a regiment.

We are adding to the defensive strength of Newbern. Rumor has it that the rebels are in strong force at Kinston. The situation of affairs in Virginia, and the growing importance of Gen. Foster's command, render the report more than probable. The feint of an attack, or the probability of it, has not prevented the embarkation from this place of a large expeditionary force for some point or points to us unknown, but doubtless of vital importance to the rebels. The result of its operations will reach you in good time. Unexpectedly to ourselves and to every one else, our regiment is left behind to help guard Newbern, now deemed by some the post of danger. The 45th is doing provost-guard duty in Newbern.

*   *   *

If Leigh Hunt, who discoursed so eloquently of the comforts of a bed, could have added to his genius the experience of a soldier, his bed panegyrics would have been moving indeed.[10] The leisurely process of disrobing preparatory for the smooth comfort of clean sheets may not inaptly be compared to the change from the heavy, crawling chrysalis to the winged and airy insect radiant of a new experience. I forget whether or not Leigh Hunt made some such comparison as this; but he did dilate upon the positive luxury springing from the contact of two legs—to wit, your own two legs—after a day's cruel separation by the nether integuments[11] which custom has rendered indispensable. If we survive our term of service, shall we not enjoy a bed? With limbs and trunks that have not pressed a sheet for nine months—limbs subjected to an intermitting friction of coarse flannel night and day for three-fourths of a year, in frigid bivouac and unyielding bunks—we certainly shall be prepared to experience and sing the pleasures of a bed when at last we come to the enjoyment of that luxury.

The Fry has arrived with our boxes.[12] Besides the many containing good things to eat were several filled with not less useful offerings in the shape of stockings, wristers, sleeping caps, &c, made and contributed by some of our young friends of the gentler sex, who accompanied their gifts with anonymous notes, or notes bearing the signatures of "Betsey Baker" and other mythical young women. Contrary to newspaper rules the editor of this paper must allow me to take notice of these communications.

"Betsey Baker" writes:

"May these socks prove a safeguard against all bullets. If they prove such inform" &c., &c.

Thank you, dear, I will.

"Nelly Bly" writes:

"Would that I were with you to darn your socks for you! If you want me to come, send" &c., &c.

"Mary of the Wild Moor" writes:

"Will the receiver of these socks please send me an account of the first march he takes with them?"

This letter was commenced on board the transport steamer Northerner, an old lake boat, which is now transporting the 44th Regiment from Newbern to Plymouth, N.C. The Northerner is a spacious, comfortable old craft, and we are far better commoded on board of her than we were on the Merrimac, which conveyed us from Boston, or the George C Collins, which afterwards carried us to Washington and then back to Newbern from Plymouth. Some of us really rejoice in the possession of staterooms, but the majority are contented to stretch themselves upon the floors of the spacious and well-lighted saloons, where at night we lie at every angle, and sleep like bricks. The stores by the Fry and other arrivals are serving us a good purpose while we are away from the comforts of the barracks. We haven't our daily soft bread, fresh meat and coffee twice a day, but our knapsacks are filled with preserved meats and fruits, apples, cakes, cheese, butter, &c., and the craving for food born of sea air is more than satisfied. Our regular rations of hard tack and salt meat at the bottom of our haversacks will keep until we need them.

We like these occasional aquatic trips. They are so good for the health and spirits of the men, that we half suspect our excellent surgeon had a voice in the planning of this last expedition. Newbern is hardly desirable as a place of long-continued residence, although an admirable and easily-defended military post. The band (our band) are with us, with their instruments. Their muskets are at Newbern, hence I conclude our expedition is not intended to be a very sanguinary one.

FEBRUARY 2, 1863.

We arrived at Plymouth about half past three this afternoon, and were glad to be informed that we were to retain our comfortable quarters on board the steamer until the next day. The cooks went on shore and made us coffee, and we supped comfortably. The evening opened beautifully, with a singularly bright moon, and the boys were in high spirits. Groups gathered upon the deck and sung glees. The saloon was cleared for a dance, and the light fantastic was tripped to the music of two fifes. The band took a position upon the hurricane deck, and discoursed their best strains. About the fires on the shore were groups of agile contrabands, delighting a number of spectators with their unique dances and songs. Altogether, a more cheering and picturesque scene could not well be imagined.

FEBRUARY 3, 1863.

We awoke this morning to find the ground white with snow, and the air thick with flakes, driven by a high wind. The scene was decidedly New Englandish, and contrasted curiously with that of the preceding evening. The climate of the "Sunny South" is certainly not without its freaks. We shall remain on board to-day, we are happy to be informed.

Plymouth shows sad marks of the recent rebel raid upon that town. Nearly fifty houses were burned by them, and the court-house, where our little force rallied, is thickly marked with their artillery shots. Upon our arrival the place was garrisoned by two companies of the Massachusetts 27th, one of the 3d, and a small force of North Carolina [Union] Cavalry. Three or four gunboats are also here, and it is rumored that we are to act in concert with them in an attack upon Rainbow Bluff, where a North Carolina regiment (the 17th, the same which we routed at Rawle's Mill, on the third of November) is said to be strongly entrenched. Rainbow Bluff commands the Roanoke River, a very few miles this side of Hamilton, and over thirty miles from Plymouth. We find here a North Carolina deserter who sets the rebel loss at Kinston at five hundred. The rebel skedaddle from that place was of the most confused description. We are gratified to learn, as we do from the same sources, that we did the rebels serious detriment at Whitehall, a fact which their hidden position would not permit us to know at the time. The enemy had an excellent view of us, and their riflemen were ordered to make General Stevenson, whom they recognized, a particular mark.[13]

We remained at Plymouth yesterday. The right wing of the regiment was transferred from the steamer to a large storehouse on the wharf. It was a cold day and we had no fires in the building, so the boys wandered over the town, and made themselves comfortable in negro cabins, where they boiled their coffee and ate hoe-cake and other luxuries.

The right snug hostelry of Mary Lee, a free colored woman and an excellent cook, was the centre of attraction, being thronged with officers, naval and military, all day. Your correspondent and a friend or two were happy enough to sit at a Christian table for almost the first time since leaving Boston, and devour fried pork and eggs, white biscuits, etc. To make our happiness complete, our frames were last night pillowed upon a Northern feather bed. It was a terribly cold night for North Carolina, and we had reason to bless the fate which gave us a warm bed in place of the cold, cheerless old storehouse where most of the boys shivered the night through.

Last evening, after supper, we sat by the cheerful fireside of a North Carolina Unionist, and while we watched the blaze between the jambs, listened with a charmed sense to the tinkle of the tea things as they were washed and set away. Our host, hostess, and two youngest occupied a bed in the warmest corner of the sitting room, "Goff, the Regicide,"[14] John and your correspondent slept in the opposite corner. We retired first, but were not too sleepy to watch with thrilling interest the series of comforting preparations before a domestic couple with a baby can retire. The infant was in its happiest mood; and, while its little limbs were allowed to bask in the firelight, it held a crooning conversation with its father, who assured the offspring that it was a right smart baby and had slept a heap since morning.

It is now high noon of Wednesday. A facetious fellow, one of the heroes of Tarboro', has just informed me that the "object of the expedition (to Plymouth) is accomplished," and that "Plymouth" is to be put upon our banner.

FEBRUARY 8, 1863.

On our way back to Newbern, when, in my last, I gave currency to the rumor that the object of our expedition to Plymouth was accomplished, I only gave echo to a popular mistake. But yesterday noon an order from headquarders [sic], addressed to our right wing, directing us to put ourselves in light marching order, with twenty-four hours' rations of hard tack in our haversacks, gave us a renewed impression of the uncertainty of camp rumors, and told us unmistakably that something was on foot. In the morning Colonel Lee had given us the liberty of the town, and the enthusiasm with which this favor had been received and enjoyed was not a little dampened by the unexpected order, which many of us received while delectating ourselves at the tables spread for us by the natives of Plymouth. What was up? Where were we to go? "Into the bush for wood," remarked our always complaisant Quartermaster, "and perhaps a little farther, to stretch your legs, if the roads are not too heavy." As though the heroes of Tarboro' and Goldsboro' needed to have their legs stretched! We noted suspiciously the twinkle in the eye of the Quartermaster, but fell in at the word of command, and were soon marching out of Plymouth on the "Long Acre Road."[15]

A mile or two out the road forked. Here we left Co. B and half of Co. C to act as picket guards on each avenue. Leaving the Washington road on our right, and soon after our wagons by a pile of dry wood, we found ourselves repeating the old familiar tramp, tramp through the mud and sand and water of North Carolina, past weather-stained but comfortable looking homesteads; past small plantations, through pine woods, through creeks, and over bridges. We were not long in ascertaining the fact that we were on a foraging expedition, and if history should call it a reconnoisance, the misnomer will never restock the stables and storehouses, the bee-hives and hen-roosts, that night depleted along the road of Long Acre. We received an early hint that we were going to capture a lot of bacon, twelve miles out of Plymouth, but if the residents along the road this side that point managed to save their own bacon and things, they certainly had reason to bless their stars. If it would not be considered unsoldierly and too sentimental, your correspondent might feel inclined to deprecate this business of foraging, as it is carried on. It is pitiful to see homes once, perhaps, famed for their hospitality, entered and robbed; even if the robbers respect the code of war. It is not less hard for women and children to be deprived of the means of subsistence because their husbands and sons and brothers are shooting at us from the bush. But war is a great, a terrible, an undiscriminating monster, and no earthly power may stay the ravages of the unleashed brute.

Ten miles from Plymouth we were forced to wade nearly knee deep through a creek one-fourth of a mile wide at the ford. The water was ice-cold, and gave our feet and ankles a pain more intense than I can well describe. At last (about half past ten o'clock) we halted, and were happy to be informed that the object of the expedition was accomplished. The column was near a house. After making somewhat particular inquiries we were informed that we had captured a dozen barrels of pork, and that the chaplain, as a temperance measure, had resolutely knocked in the head of a barrel of sweet cider, but not, however, until a few enterprising fellows had filled their canteens with the delicious beverage. We were now ready to countermarch, and five o'clock this morning found us again at Plymouth, after a night march of twenty-five miles.

But for the risk of being tedious, I would ask the reader to accompany us upon our return, to halt with us at every house and listen to the voice of disturbed poultry aroused from sleep to die an untimely death; to see the column halt at every henery, and promptly move again when the victimized fowls had given utterance to their last despairing notes; to see donkey carts laden with geese upset in the creek, and hear the eloquently profane protests of officers and privates as they again floundered through the ice-water at the long ford. It was a rough night, but all experience is valuable.

We lay still a portion of last night and this forenoon in Albemarle Sound, on account of fog. This afternoon we were obliged to take coal, and at nightfall, a mile off Roanoke Island, the fog was again setting in. We shall probably not reach Newbern until late to-morrow. This letter will be taken to Roanoke Island, and go from thence to New York.

* * *

Newbern, N.C.

FEB. 17, 1863.

We are visited occasionally at Newbern by friends from Boston. Few things are more agreeable to us than the sight of forms and faces bringing with them airs of home. We scan the dress of a civilian as something almost *outre* for its singularity. The sight of smooth, white shirts is positively tantalizing. Among our visitors here have been J. Thomas Stevenson and wife, father and mother of General Stevenson, Rev. Mr. [Charles F.] Barnard, Rev. Mr. [James W.] Thompson, of Jamaica Plain, and Rev. Dr. [Samuel K.] Lothrop.[16] The latter gentleman preached to the regiment on the 15th. To gaze upon the goodly rotundity of that familiar form was like being introduced to a slice of Boston, whereof the centre was the old church and cannon ball in Brattle Square. He favored us with an admirable discourse from the words, "Keep thy heart with all diligence, for out of it are the issues of life." No admonition is more needed by the soldier than that conveyed in this text, and as enforced by the energetic eloquence of Dr. Lothrop. We need frequent reminders of the justness and greatness of our cause to keep our hearts warmly engaged in a service so full of sacrifice as this. I fear we have too little of the martyr-spirit which saves a people, and that the North must make up in numbers and treasure what it lacks in the heroic spirit of the fathers of the Revolution. If our nice young gentlemen at home hope to keep clear of this scrape, I fear they will be disappointed.

Among our visitors from Boston, I should have mentioned Sergeant [George W.] Wheelwright, who came out as supercargo of the schooner Fry. The reception which his friends in the regiment extended to him was of the most touching description. After numerous affectionate embraces, he was invited to take a drink—of quinine! This being declined, hard tack and salt horse were severally pressed upon him with an urgent hospitality difficult to be refused. Upon our late expedition from Plymouth (named the *ham-fat*), Sergeant Wheelwright acted as orderly for Colonel Lee, and showed himself a forager of great natural ability. As we witnessed him first mounted upon a dashing mule, and then a fleet horse, we could hardly persuade ourselves that he had not profited by the rich experiences of Tarboro' and Goldsboro'.

Among the few deaths which have recently occurred in the regiment is that of private [Francis C.] Hopkinson, of Company F, who died of typhoid fever. He was a graduate of Harvard College, and one of the brightest intellects in the regiment. A few years ago he was temporarily connected with the Boston Advertiser. His remains have been embalmed, and will be sent North.

We are beginning to feel the breath of spring. Dandelions are commencing to bloom in Newbern, and wild onions are springing up over our parade ground. At night the neighboring swamps are vocal with the voices of frogs.

We are to have a dramatic entertainment with which to celebrate the anniversary of Washington's birth-day, provided, of course, we are allowed to remain in Newbern. At present our brigade is a divided one, the Connecticut 10th and the Massachusetts 24th being a part of the great Southern expedition. General Stevenson is with the 10th and 24th. The remaining regiment of our brigade, the Rhode Island 5th, is with us at Newbern.

* * *

We celebrated Washington's birthday on the evening of the 23d by a *bal masque* in the barracks of Companies D and E. The affair crowned and surpassed all our previous efforts in this line, and was universally decided to be a big thing. The barracks, which had recently been whitewashed, were united by the removal of a partition, and formed a saloon one hundred and twenty feet in length. The fronts of the bunks were covered with shelter tents depending like curtains. To these at proper intervals were attached scrolls with green borders bearing the names of the captains and lieutenants of the regiment. More conspicuously appeared the names of Colonel Lee and staff, General Stevenson, of our brigade, General Wessells, of our division, and General Foster, chief of this army corps. At the head of the saloon was erected a platform carpeted with rubber blankets. Back of this was suspended a large American flag, with the name of Washington upon a scroll. Upon other scrolls appeared the date of his birth and the words "First in war," &c. Midway of the barracks was graceful canopy of flags, and at various other points the national colors were appropriately disposed to heighten the general effect. Our well-burnished rifles were crossed on the front of the bunks, and rayed from centers on the walls. Chandeliers, beautifully trimmed with green and moss, lighted up the long room and its decorations, and gave the apartment an appearance of real magnificence. It even surpassed the most sanguine expectations of those who had industriously labored upon the decorations. Such was the appearance of the barracks alone; but when later in the evening they were crowded with people wearing the varied and grotesque costumes of the occasion, and the uniforms of a large number of officers, the scene was more brilliant than I can describe.

But the chief feature of the occasion was the presence of General Foster, General Wessells, and a large number of officers from various regiment in this department, all of whom were pleased to warmly commend the taste and enterprise of the 44th boys. It is needless to say that the presence of our distinguished visitors was enthusiastically recognized by us.

The following was the order of dances:—

1. March and Sicilian Circle   Lee's Quickstep.
2. Quadrille   Sullivan's Double Quick.
3. Les Lancers   Richardson's March.
4. Contra   Skittletop Gallop.
5. Polka Redowa   Odiorne's Choice.
6. Quadrille   Surgeon's Call.
7. Polka   Mary Lee's Delight.
8. Contra   Stebbins's Reel.

INTERMISSION.

Waltz—Varsovienne—Schottische.

9. Quadrille   Ham Fat Man.
10. Waltz   Pas de Seul.
11. Quadrille   Dismal Swamp Promenade.
12. Contra   Our Friends at Home.
13. Polka Quadrille   Long Acre Gallop.
14. Quadrille   Dug-out Race.
15. Military do   Newell's March.

Here is the managerial card:

GRAND MASQUERADE BALL

Sir:—The pleasure of your company, with ladies, is respectfully solicited at a Grand Bal Masque to be given under the auspices of the 44th Regimental Dramatic Association, at the Barracks of Companies D and E, on MONDAY EVENING, FEB. 23, 1863.

The management desire to state that nothing will be left undone to render it the party of the season.

Floor Managers.
Willard Howard. J. B. Rice. Harry T. Reed.
Committee of Arrangements.

Sergeant	G. L. Tripp,	Company	D.
"	H. A. Homer,	"	E.
Corporal	Z. T. Haines,	"	D.
"	J. B. Gardner,	"	D.
"	J. W. Cartwright,	"	E.
"	M. E. Boyd,	"	D.
"	C. E. Tucker,	"	E.
Private	F. A. Sayer,	"	D.
"	H. Howard,	"	D.
"	J. H. Waterman, Jr.,	"	D.
"	H. Bradish,	"	E.
"	C. H. Demeritt,	"	D.
"	D. Howard,	"	D.
"	E. L. Hill,	"	A.

In order to defray the expenses, tickets will be placed at 10 cents each, to be procured of the Managers. No tickets sold at the door. Visitors are expected to appear *en costume.*

Music by the New Berne Quadrille Band, five pieces.
The Management desire to express their sincere thanks to the Officers of this Regiment for the many favors granted by them in aid of this undertaking.
The hall will be appropriately decorated.

The Newbern Quadrille Band, composed of *dis*colored young gentlemen, did not distinguish itself: but our own regimental band, under Major [George L.] Babcock,—which, by the way, has received its splendid new instruments,—came to the rescue gallantly, and added largely to the *eclat* of the affair, which, by the way, was *pecuniarily* successful, leaving us funds which will enable us to produce in good time an original opera, and one expected to contain several local and personal hits. But of that hereafter.

The following deaths have recently occurred in the regiment:

Geo. B. Young, Co. G, malarious fever.

Charles A. Bradt, Co. C, malarious fever.

E. N. Fuller, Co. A., measles.

James S. Gilmore, Co. K, diptheria [*sic*] and lung fever.

Sergt. Charles Harwood, Co. I, diptheria [*sic*].

This month fifteen men have been discharged for disability. The general health of the regiment, however, is quite good—better than it was a short time ago; but experience is convincing all concerned that our miserably pinched up barracks are a fruitful cause of disease. The regiments in tents are the healthiest ones.

The Boston regiment of colored men has excited much interest here. Some of our best men have accepted commissions in it. Among these are Lieut. [Albert S.] Hartwell, Sergts. [Garth W.] James and [Cabot J.] Russell, of Co. F. We shall part with these men with great regret, and at the same time give them a hearty Godspeed in their brave and self-sacrificing undertaking. There is no warmer friend of the Massachusetts 54th regiment than Col. Lee; and the best evidence of the fact is in the cheerful alacrity which he shows in supplying it with officers from the best men of his own command. I understand that Gen. Foster favors the scheme of recruiting regiments of colored men. Several items of regimental news must lie over.

* * *

Newbern, N.C.,

MARCH 4, 1863.

My last letter contained a brief account of a Washington birth-day ball in our barracks, but the hasty description I was then obliged to give conveyed a very inadequate idea of the brilliancy of the subject, and will be quite unsatisfactory to those who were present. I cannot remember a ball-room which presented a finer effect in its decorations than ours. It was remarkable to observe what a little taste and industry were able to accomplish with our limited means, not only as respects the decorations, but in the costumes and characters assumed. The young women who had stunned all beholders at previous masquerades, appeared with augmented charms. Some were doubtless outstripped by others, but I shall this time avoid invidious comparisons. The "Albino Family," with head-dresses of frayed ropes, was an exceedingly clever take-off of [P. T.] Barnum's curious beings at the Aquarial Gardens. Deacon Doolittle, of Vermont, who had come down to Newbern to gratify himself with the spectacle of young men bleeding for their country, was one of the richest impersonations of the evening. The old man was deeply surprised to see young ladies smoking cigars, and averred that such a thing was unheard of when he was a young man. Deacon Doolittle got interested in Deacon Foster, and the two were seen arm-in-arm. The white woolly locks and limp of the latter deacon were unmistakable in the throng. Deacon Doolittle's humanitarian character having got noised about among the managers, the old man was invited to the platform, from which he made an edifying address, at last bringing down the house by kissing a gun which he held in his hand.

Among other assumptions were those of a member of the Howard street, [Boston], blackleg fraternity, "The Press," a harlequin, several devils, &c., &c. "The Press" was clad in newspapers, the Sunday Herald being conspicuous among a great variety of enterprising journals displayed in the costume. Several rollicking sailors and dashing cavalry officers gave variety to the costumes and added life to the scene. The little brigadier of Company A was admirably made up, and the character was sustained in a manner truly artistic. The same may be said of the little Continental brigadier of Company E, the Indian, of the same company, the Turk, of Company F, and Miss Columbia, of Company C, who, being the "Gem of the Ocean," was observed to be on intimate terms with one of the sailors. Some of our friends will have the pleasure of examining pictures of several of these characters, and will thus obtain a better idea of their appearance than it is possible for me to give in words, even if I should undertake the hopeless task.

Last Wednesday, the 25th, witnessed a grand review of the troops at Newbern. Our friends may be pleased to know that the 44th Regiment was generally acknowledged to be second to no regiment in the field for the excellence of its marching and general appearance. The review was witnessed by a large number of spectators, including many ladies in carriages and on horseback.

Day before yesterday Companies F and B, Captains [Samuel] Storrow and [John M.] Griswold, were sent out to do picket duty a few miles up the railroad.

The last death in our regiment was that of Otis S. Merrill, of Company C, who died of measles. Nearly fifty are on the sick list. There are but few cases of malarious fever among our men, but the Massachusetts 51st has suffered quite severely from it. That regiment is soon to commence garrison duty at Beaufort and Fort Macon, the Paradise of this department. The 44th will probably soon do provost marshal duty in Newbern.

*   *   *

Newbern, N.C.,

MARCH 14, 1863.

The peaceful quiet of our life at Newbern was to-day interrupted by an attack from the rebels. Gen. Foster had arranged to celebrate the day in a manner becoming the anniversary of the capture of Newbern. But a grand march in review and other *et ceteras* were unexpectedly substituted by salutes with shot and shell from a brigade of rebels on the eastern shore of the Neuse, who made an early attack upon our outpost on that shore. This outpost force, which is stationed directly opposite the camp of our regiment, consisted of the New York 92nd regiment, strongly entrenched near the shore. Previous to the attack, the rebel General [James Johnston Pettigrew] is reported to have sent in several demands for a surrender, which were promptly refused. The rebels then commenced a vigorous fire of grape and canister, which passed harmlessly over the heads of the little garrison, and beat the waters of the Neuse into foam. An occasional shell from the rebel lines came over the river and lodged upon our parade ground; and groups of spectators from our regiment, standing upon the shore, were admonished not to present too conspicuous a mark for the enemy's artillery. After a while, the rebels, observing the inefficacy of their fire, as the story goes about camp, attempted to carry our works by storm, but without result, save in a serious loss from the volleys which met their approach. In the meanwhile, several of our gunboats were doing good service by landing shells at proper places, and feeling up and down shore with their iron fingers. Several field batteries were also set at work on either side of our barracks, and by noon the rebel artillery was silenced.[17]

Of course the air is full of rumors, to wit: immense force of rebels on every side; rebel generals swear they will dine at the Gaston House to-morrow; pickets driven in or captured on the Neuse and Trent roads; Beaufort and Roanoke captured; the railroad seized; more fighting to-night, &c., &c. That our pickets have been disturbed is doubtless true. Artillery and infantry have been sent out on the great roads, and over the Neuse the picket force is augmented, and great vigilance is for some good reason exercised. I shall not be able to send you later advices by this departure. We are not much frightened; and, if we have got to fight the rebels, have no objections to doing so once with the advantages on our side. I allude to gunboats, plenty of ammunition, rifle pits, &c., and no long marches.

I enclose herewith the libretto of an opera written and produced by members of our regiment. If you will reprint it, it may amuse some of our friends in Boston, although its best points are more apparent to the members of the regiment than to anybody else. You will not find the music. That was improvised and selected, and very many appropriate airs and witticisms were introduced in places not indicated in the printed text. It has been publicly produced three times before large audiences (two long barracks being full each time), including officers of the highest rank in this Department. Thursday night Gen. Foster and staff, with his wife and nearly all the Northern ladies now resident in Newbern, were present.[18] With the body of the house filled by officers in full uniform, opera has rarely been honored by a more brilliant audience. We had a spacious stage, an act-drop, and other scenery, foraged from an old theatre in Newbern, some scenery painted by our own artists, a profusion of flags and green decorations, and a beautiful tableau with blue-lights to close with. The orchestra, under the lead of Mr. [Charles E.] Hooke, played splendidly, and with a truly theatrical effect. Altogether, our distinguished auditors expressed themselves not only remarkably pleased with our efforts, but greatly surprised at what we had been able to accomplish under the circumstances of our position. Last night we gave an entertainment to the invalid guards of the Connecticut 10th and the Massachusetts 24th, the two detached regiments of our brigade, and one hundred men from the Rhode Island 5th. A thousand copies of the libretto have been printed, and their sale has added a handsome amount to the charitable fund of the regiment.

MARCH 15.

The night was peaceful. Our extra pickets have come in, and the rebels are believed to have skedaddled. It is probable that their main purpose was to capture our outpost on the east side of the Neuse, but, failing in this, have retreated. The rebels will always find Newbern a hot place.

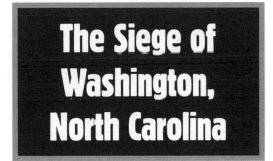

CHAPTER 7

The Siege of Washington, North Carolina

Washington, N.C.,

MARCH 16, 1863.

We bid fair to get the name of the "expeditionary regiment" of this department. You will observe by the date of this letter that we have again pulled up stakes at Newbern, and moved to Washington, at the head of Pamlico Sound. Our friends will want an explanation of this new movement. My last letter mentioned an unsuccessful rebel attack on our outpost on the easterly side of the Neuse. We were afterwards informed by negroes and deserters that seven hundred rebels were engaged in this attack, and that eight thousand were at the same time moving down on the Trent road, where they were promptly held in check by infantry and artillery sent out by General Foster. It is quite probable that these figures were not far from correct.[1] That the rebels were in large force at Kinston has been well understood ever since our return from the Goldsboro' raid, and they probably thought to make an easy conquest of the little force over the Neuse, well knowing that it would form a very pretty little celebration of the anniversary of the capture of Newbern. But failing in this project, as well as in their attempt to plant batteries with which to shell the town, the rebel forces withdrew. But it was a matter of some doubt with General Foster whether the rebels would return to Kinston without attempting to accomplish something in this direction. He therefore determined to strengthen the garrison at Washington by sending hither our regiment, minus companies F and B, on picket, and here we are. We left Newbern last evening by the fine new little steamer Escort, and after a pleasant trip arrived here this afternoon. We came up to the wharf with music and flying colors, creating by our advent no little sensation among the soldiers and contrabands who came dancing down to the river in flocks. The afternoon sun was shining briskly, and Washington presented a very lively and attractive air. We find eight companies of the Massachusetts 27th here, two companies of the North Carolina [Union] regiment, a company of cavalry and a company of artillery. The town is admirably protected by earthworks, block houses and a formidable fort, to say nothing of three gunboats in the stream. Nevertheless, a rebel attack seems to be anticipated. Colonel Lee, of our regiment, in command of the detached brigade, formed by the Massachusetts 44th and the Rhode Island 5th, assumes command of this post. Tonight we bivouac a little west of the town upon the famous Grist plantation. We are occupying shelter tents for the first time, and find them "quite bully." The rapidity with which our canvas village assumed shape was amazing. The boys are assembled about the bivouac fires in high sport, or reading or writing by the light of candles within the tents. Colonel Lee has delighted all hearts by taking possession of the Grist mansion as his headquarters. The loyalty of its proprietor is said to be of such an uncertain character that Colonel Lee has decided to put a little wholesome restriction upon his future movements. His house and grounds are the most elegant we have seen in North Carolina, and his cellar is said to be well stored with apple-jack. Grist himself is a fat, impudent looking specimen of the race of secesh.

While we were standing about the fires this morning waiting for our coffee, we received a hurried order to strike tents. We had no doubt that, in consequence of important news from the pickets, a march was in contemplation, but were soon agreeably disappointed to ascertain that we were only required to pitch our tents so as to form company streets. Upon this job we then entered with alacrity.

Grist (who is profanely misnamed by the soldiers) packed up his goods this morning preparatory to moving to his suburban residence outside our lines; but Colonel Lee decided that he couldn't dispense with his fascinating society at this juncture, especially as Governor Stanley's [sic] passport is no longer valuable to Grist or any other of the Governor's rebel favorites. Grist submitted philosophically. His mansion looms up temptingly among the trees near the right of our line. The place, I am told, figured in Porte Crayon's North Carolina sketches; but the mansion has been renovated since then.[2] It has doubtless been one of many hospitable homes in Washington, which place is said to have been famed for its hospitality.

This afternoon we were startled from our siestas by the metallic crack of rifled cannon on one of the gunboats. It was a charming sound,—scarcely less so than the dulcet strains of the 44th band, which at the present moment is discoursing "Departed Days" at Colonel Lee's headquarters. They were feeling for rebels in the woods on the south side of the river. Scouts sent over the bridge last night and to-day report the presence of the enemy's pickets and intrenchments two or three miles up the road.

No further sign of the enemy. After spending most of a very warm day in listlessness, we were marched through the town this evening for a dress parade with the 27th, upon the spot where we bivouaced last fall. The dust was intolerable, and the "expedition" was generally regarded as a non-paying one. It afforded us, however, a good view of the town and its inhabitants. The female portion of the latter are not remarkable for smiling countenances. As a rule they are not lively, being either podgy, with turn-up noses, or bony and forlorn. They talk through their noses.

MARCH 20.

Your correspondent assisted in the performance of picket duty last night. The weather was terribly severe. For some reason or other an attack was momentarily expected, and we were kept upon the *qui vive*. When we returned this morning, benumbed and drenched to the skin with rain, we found the infantry all behind the earthworks ready for action. It is now night, but there are no signs of the enemy.

* * *

Washington, N.C.,
MARCH 20, 1863.

Our late exposure upon picket duty, and the continued rain, induced our officers to mercifully permit us to leave our shelter tents, and occupy houses in town, so to-night we find ourselves happy in the enjoyment of excellent shelter and warm fires. What a contrast with our situation last night out on the Tarboro' road, drenched to the skin and chilled to the centre! The liberty of the town has enabled us to fortify ourselves with such dainties as ham and eggs, milk, &c., and we are now as comfortable as heart could wish. Better than all, we are not likely to be disturbed to-night, for our cavalry scouts bring intelligence of the withdrawal of the rebels from this vicinity.

Near where our shelter tents are pitched is the humble domicil of Aunt Fanny and family, members of the patriarchal household of Grist.[3] Fanny's fireside was a great centre of attraction, and about it the soldiers crowded in scores to escape the rain, against which cotton houses proved a slim protection. Aunt Fanny is of a retiring disposition, and it required the exercise of unusual energy on her part to keep one little place at the fire for herself and children. She must have shared our joy, but for another reason, when we were ordered to take up our abode in town. While we remained in her vicinity, all she could do was to fortify herself with snuff, of which she is a veteran "dipper." Our presence must have caused a large consumption of this consoling article. She transferred the snuff from a tin box to her mouth with a sweet gum wood stick, which she used like a tooth brush, and then left the handle sticking out of her mouth. Aunt Fanny afforded me the first opportunity I ever had of witnessing the operation of "dipping," and I am thus particular in my reference to this classic custom, which is said to prevail among the white women as well as the black ones at the South. Aunt Fanny's sombre face and the protruding handle of the gum stick would form a fit subject for the pencil of Porte Crayon. While I witnessed, with a twinge of sympathy, Aunt Fanny's patient sufferance of the invasion of her castle, I could not but wish that some good fairy would suddenly endow her with the momentum and muscular power of the shoulder-hitting *Charity*, empress of the Newbern washerwomen, who submits to no nonsense, but lays about her, right and left, according to the number of those who provoke her just wrath by unseemly liberties.

MARCH 21.

Last night the Thespians of the 27th Regiment performed "The Irish Tutor" and "Michael Earle." They have fitted up a little theatre, and furnished it with an act-drop, scenery, &c., of their own painting. Our own dramatic corps are quite unhappy to find Washington without a suitable opera house. It is proposed when we get back to Newbern to produce Dr. Jones's "Solon Shingle," if the public demand for more opera is not too clamorous. The musical world will be glad to know that the organs of our principal singers are as yet unaffected by the severe trials of picket duty; a fact the more noticeable, perhaps, considering that those organs have not been lubricated with whisky rations from first to last of our severe trials as soldiers. It won't do for soldiers to murmur in public, but you can fancy our feelings!

It is assumed by our naval men here that the rebels have two gunboats up the Tar River. This is probably correct. The building of a gunboat at Tarboro' was among the supposed reasons for our attempted expedition to that place last November. Very little fear of them, however, exists. It is imagined by some that the rebels will come down upon this place in scows. That route would please us.

We find the colored population here quite fearful of an attack, and many of them with their effects packed up preparatory to a hurried removal to boats. Among these is Henrietta, a very nice young woman, the slave of a Unionist, who cooks excellent dinners for a few of us hungry fellows, in a snug, white-washed cabin at the east end of the town. Henrietta is as neat, intelligent and lady-like as the average of white women. Her bondage, if such it can be called, sits lightly upon her; but she has no sympathy for rebels, and like many others here, severely denounces the sutlers who, for the sake of making money, furnish the secessionists of this region with food and clothing. Henrietta rejoices in the possession of an excellent cow, a *rara avis* in North Carolina. The peach trees in her garden have put on their pink dresses, and the robins, wooed by their fragrance, are trapped and murdered by Henrietta for her table. I caught the lady in this slaughtering business, and found her a little nervous about the law touching her case.

A party of us strayed into the old town hall to-day. The official papers and books were strewn all over the building without the slightest appearance of any attempt at preservation or order. While wandering through the maze, an officer attached to the permanent garrison of the place appeared before us, and sharply ordered us away from the premises. We [of] course obeyed, but thought his exercise of authority was in poor keeping with the utter neglect and destruction which had already been allowed to mark the building and its contents.

Went to a negro church to-day in an old building not long since used as a theatre, the fresco and gilding still remaining about the proscenium. The preacher and his chief men and women sat upon the stage, the bulk of the audience, including several soldiers, in front. The singing was congregational, and line by line, as it was read by the preacher. It was horrible. The praying and preaching better appealed to the emotions. We certainly were not unmoved by the earnest petition in behalf of the "soldiers of the North who had given them their liberty," by the prayers for the welfare of our friends at home, and for victory over our enemies. The sermon was an invocation for watchfulness, with copious illustrations from military experience. It was rich in funny logic and quaint grammar.

After a three days' equinoctial storm, the sun is out cheeringly this afternoon.

There is a boat in from Newbern this morning, and the indications are that our ten days' absence is to be indefinitely extended. All the companies but D and H, who are housed near our camp-ground, are ordered back to the shelter tents. "Bully for D and H" is the general sentiment.

Horace P. Tuttle, the soldier-astronomer of our regiment, has been appointed assistant paymaster in the navy. He has not fully decided to accept the unexpected and unsolicited honor, and we hope he may remain with his many friends of the 44th through its term of service.

I think I have not mentioned in this or my previous letter from Washington that but eight of our companies are here. Companies B and F, Captains Griswold and Storrow, were left behind doing picket duty on the railroad a few miles above Newbern.

* * *

Washington, N.C.,

MARCH 24, 1863.

We are not much in love with this Washington, N.C. It seems too much like "some banquet hall deserted." We suspect it of insalubrity. We don't like "the folks." We shall be glad when we strike tents. But while we remain here we propose to avail ourselves of all mitigating circumstances. Last evening, John Smith, banjoist, came to our quarters at the Pamlee mansion. His instrument was made of an old sieve and a pine stick, but in volume and sweetness of tone, I don't remember to have heard it surpassed. Of course it set all the niggers to dancing, especially our old friend and favorite, West Williams, who earned new laurels in the light fantastic. John Smith, besides being a splendid banjoist, has a voice like a robin.

To-day the lines have been open, and the women of the suburbs have been thronging into town to buy a little sugar, coffee, snuff, &c., especially snuff. Our friend Grist has at last been permitted to go outside the lines. He doesn't attempt to disguise a degree of sympathy with the Southern cause, but his outward conduct towards us has been gentlemanly.

Contrabands report a large rebel force (seven thousand) within seven miles of Washington, one day last week; and that they were restrained from advancing on the place by hearing that the garrison was reinforced. If this is true, "the object of the expedition is accomplished," and we may expect to return to Newbern very soon. One of the officers of the permanent garrison here has taken a Southern woman for a wife. They are our next door neighbors. As we see them together, planting flowers in the door-yard, we fancy we might become reconciled even to Washington, N.C., under such circumstances. There is a call now upon the gardening skill of the regiment, and some of the boys have voluntarily ornamented the vicinity of their shelter-tents with plants in full bloom.

Washington, N.C., in its palmy days, is described as "a hard old place." It was a slave market of some consequence, and the population consumed a good deal of "ardent spirits," according to the authority of a venerable "aunty" who lives in a cabin attached to our quarters. Street duels were a common affair. An election was considered tame without two or three attendant rows and stabbings. The poor white people left behind here, and even those of respectable appearance, are unable to read or write. They considered it unlawful to send their children to school—so says a decent looking woman whose husband is an unwilling soldier in the rebel army. The more we learn of the despicable social condition of the South, the stronger appears the need of the purification which, in the Providence of God, comes of the fire and the sword.

MARCH 25.

While Company K was quartered in town they were directly opposite a house inhabited with others by a comely young woman, who so excited the admiration of a susceptible young man in the company that he was impelled to send her a love missive. It was in good set terms, smelling strongly of "The Ready Letter-Writer," but the young lady was so little moved by its elegance, that she returned the note with a resentful addendum, threatening to tell the Colonel, and expressing a wish to have no communication with her "enemies."

A gunboat came in from Newbern last night, increasing the fleet to four. We have a fine bracing air to-day, and the health of the regiment is excellent. We are also made happy by a mail from the North containing bills of lading, which means boxes for us at Newbern.

I learn to-day that Plymouth has again been menaced by the rebels, but that the prompt arrival of reinforcements saved the place. Gen. Foster is never caught napping. An increasing confidence is entertained for his generalship.

* * *

Washington, N.C.,

MARCH 30, 1863.

Yesterday completed the first seven months of our service as volunteer soldiers, dating from the time we went into camp at Readville as a full, organized regiment. Whether our term of service commenced on the 29th of August or on the 12th of September, when we were formally mustered into service, is not yet definitely announced; but we incline to the opinion that we shall be held for nine months from the latter date. It has been rumored that we are to be detained for nine months from the time that we received marching orders, late in October, but we have little fear of that. It is needless to say that almost every man in the regiment is looking fondly forward to his emancipation from the restraints, deprivations, and hardships of military life to the reunion of hearts and the enjoyment of home comforts.

Yesterday I again attended worship at a colored church, and afterward proceeded with the congregation to a baptism in the river. The sacred ordinance was characterized by entire decorum. The blacks here, who comprise a great majority of the resident population of Washington, are extremely fervent in their prayers for the success of the Northern cause, and rightly attribute their enlarged liberty to the presence of our soldiers. They are a more intelligent and orderly population than can be shown in the foreign precincts of our great cities. The only black man here who disturbs the peace is "Crazy Willis." He perambulates the streets incessantly, swearing that the war must be stopped, and that no more Yankees shall be killed. His harangues present a curious blending of profanity and pious exhortation. He was formerly a preacher of more than usual fluency. He is a very unpopular member of society, his black brethren not giving him credit for much insanity [sanity].

Gen. Foster and staff arrived here this morning, and reinforcements are said to be close by. Whether this means additional defence or another expedition I cannot say at this writing.

P.M. This forenoon a scouting party, consisting of Companies A and G, with a few cavalrymen and one piece of artillery, crossed the bridge and proceeded up the road about two miles, when they were suddenly arrested by rebels in ambush. Company G were acting as skirmishers, and advanced to within a few feet of the rebels' hiding place before receiving their fire. The result was disastrous. Three of Co. G's men were brought down and left upon the ground at the narrow defile where the rebels were posted. Capt. James Richardson, of Co. A, received two bullets in the left arm. No bones were broken. Upon receiving the fire, our men were ordered to seek cover on either side of the road, which they did until they deemed it safe to rally and return to town.

Those left dead or wounded are Orderly Sergt. [David K.] Hobart, Corporal [Theodore J.] Lawrence and John Leonard, all of Co. G. Corporal [John] King of the same company was slightly wounded by a buck-shot in the back of the head.[4] Lieut. [Frederic] Odiorne's clothes were riddled with bullets and buck-shot, as were those of Corporal [John D.] Priest. One of the latter's hands was grazed by a projectile. Others had equally narrow escapes.

MARCH 31.

We spent last night behind the breastworks, sleeping in our blankets and watching by turns. It rained almost incessantly, and we were drenched to the skin. Toward morning we were allowed to spend an hour in one of the block-houses with the boys of Co. B, Mass. 27th; but we passed most of this forenoon in the mud behind the breastworks, with no other consolation than coffee and hard tack. The gunboats and fort were firing into the woods all night, to prevent the erection of batteries. At daylight our attention was arrested by sharp musketry firing over the river. We afterwards learned that a battalion of North Carolina troops, under Capt. [C. A.] Lyon, had been sent over to prevent the erection of rebel batteries at Point Rodman, a short distance below, and that they succeeded in their purpose by smart skirmishing, in which several of their men were wounded.

APRIL 1.

The rebels lay low yesterday, and the night was peaceful; but before morning they succeeded in planting one or more formidable batteries commanding the river below, and this morning they opened on the town and our gunboats. To make matters worse, a strong west wind was driving the water out of the river, leaving our gunboats aground. This left the Hull badly exposed to the guns of the first rebel fort, and they played into her in a lively manner, dismounting two of her guns and wounding two or three of her men. The guns of the Hull, however, were not idle, but blazed away until her ammunition was exhausted. The Louisiana and Eagle were also busy during the day, but to-night no guns are heard on either side. Numerous rebel projectiles of the Whitworth pattern came into the town, but did no damage to speak of.[5] The wind has abated, the water has risen on the river, and the gunboats are afloat again. Dispatch boats succeeded in running the blockade yesterday and to-day.

APRIL 2.

Last night was quiet, but we busied ourselves in strengthening our defences. There are well-founded rumors of gunboats and reinforcements below the rebel forts, and distant firing is heard from down the river, suggesting the probability of other rebel forts farther down. A rebel flag is descried [reported] down the river, but otherwise there is very little to be seen or heard of the enemy. The videttes[6] think the rebels are skedaddling, and the boys are in high spirits.

Yesterday our pickets over the bridge learned from the enemy's pickets that the wounded men of Co. G, who were left in the hands of the enemy on the 31st., are doing well. None were killed. Orderly [David K.] Hobart, who was the most seriously hurt, was shot through one of the lungs.

In consequence of the weakness of our garrison, General Foster has organized a battalion of blacks to assist us behind the earthworks. We have no such enthusiastic soldiers in the department as they. They begged the privilege of having guns placed in their hands, and almost quarrelled for the preference. They swear they will sell their lives as dearly as possible. We are indebted, by the way, to a colored servant of Captain [Joseph R.] Kendall, who went beyond the lines the other day, for information of great value.

Yesterday a boat containing half a dozen persons was seen to cross the river a few hundred yards west of the extreme left of our line of earthworks, and land upon a point running from this shore. A six-pounder in the block-house was trained upon them, and sent them scattering in double quick time. Some of us have a troublesome suspicion that the boat's crew were deserters or contrabands. If they were rebels, their audacity is unexplainable.

To-day one of our videttes reports seeing a man suspended by the neck to an apple-tree beyond our lines. He made a careful examination with a glass, and saw a rebel officer and several privates engaged in lowering and dragging away the body, which was probably that of a man suspected of disloyalty to the rebel cause. Such is rebel justice.[7]

APRIL 3.

Another quiet night last night, although in the evening the principal rebel fort down the river fired several shots at what we surmised was a transport or gunboat coming up. Our conjecture was probably correct, as to-day we learn that fresh supplies of ammunition had been received. We are told that three regiments and two gunboats, from Newbern, are a few miles down the river, also more rebel batteries, and one of them so buried in the ground as to be unassailable by anything save mortars. Yesterday the block-house on our extreme right was a particular mark for rebel cannon. Very little damage was done, but a large gun taken from a gunboat and placed at the block-house was believed to be doing a good business. Some of the large rebel guns near the shore have been withdrawn, and one knocked out of position. Our gunboats have been firing at frequent intervals, all day to-day, although the rebels opened the ball in the morning.

P.M. We hear that five gunboats are down the river, and that while they were engaging the rebel batteries, a dispatch schooner sailed up past them. A contraband who escaped from the rebels to-day reports that we have killed "a right smart of 'em." This is very likely. A more uncertain report is that of a rebel flag of truce asking for time to bury their dead.

A vidette stationed near our block-house ventured a little too far out to-day, and exchanged shots with some rebels near a point of woods. He saw a lot of horses, mules and wagons under cover of the woods.

We are beginning to ask, "How much longer is this thing to go on?" What is the purpose of the rebels? To keep away reinforcements and provisions until they force us into a bloodless capitulation, or until they concentrate troops enough to carry our breastworks by storm? Or do they hope to draw troops enough from Newbern to leave that place exposed to capture? Or do they merely propose keeping us busy, to prevent us from sending any more troops from North Carolina for the reinforcement of the army in the Department of the South? Time only will show. We have no great apprehensions concerning the result. Our confidence in General Foster is firm and unabated. His timely presence here we regard as little less than providential.

We are still stationed close to the entrenchments which encircle the town, in shelter tents and block-houses. Company D is fortunately quartered with Company B, of the Massachusetts 27th, in block-house No. 1 and its out-buildings. We are under great obligation to them for their obliging hospitality. Their long experience has qualified them to give us many useful lessons in camp life. We watch their culinary operations with great interest, and are not a little tantalized by the sight of warm bread, flap-jacks, fried fish, &c., especially as we are now chiefly confined to hard-tack and miserable coffee.

Our black recruits are industriously drilling in marching and the manual. The favorite servants of our company, whom some of my readers will remember by the names of America and West, are exhibiting their talents as drill officers, to excellent effect. Our colored recruits are already winning golden opinions for their soldierly qualities. Our most bitter negropholists admit that they will fight, and one of their sincere haters has been detailed to officer them. Some of the poor fellows lie behind the breastworks with a spelling book in one hand and a musket in the other.

Last night was tolerably quiet, although the gunboats occasionally woke the echoes. This morning a gunboat passed the rebel batteries, and came to anchor opposite the town. She was not fired at but eight rebel guns were seen in position. There is a growing suspicion that the rebels have abandoned the siege.

9 P.M.

"A growing suspicion" has not been sustained. A reconnoisance [*sic*] was attempted to-day with a view of sounding the rebels in the vicinity of the battery on the point, but our boats were fired upon, and another artillery duel occupied the afternoon. We were again ordered behind the breastworks, but to-night are permitted to share the comfortable quarters of Company B, 27th. When we get home we propose to print in the Herald a card of thanks to Company B, after the style of the boys of Extinguisher 20, to the boys of Cataract 11—"We owe you one."[8]

APRIL 5.

The quiet of last night and this forenoon has been unbroken by the sound of guns; but this afternoon the Sunday stillness is interrupted by the solemn boom of heavy artillery down the river. Whether it proceeds from the rebel forts or our gunboats we do not know. Yesterday it was rumored that the spades were collected and sent down the river to be used in intrenching our reinforcements held back by the blockade. Certain it is, we could get no spades for our own use last night. It was rumored yesterday that the rebels were feeling about Newbern.

APRIL 6.

The rebels have been throwing up additional earthworks down the river, and seem to have entered upon the siege in earnest. The smoke of their bivouac fires increases from night to night, and it is highly probable that they are receiving reinforcements of infantry.

APRIL 8.

An attack was strongly expected night before last, and a heavy picket force was stationed all along our line of defence. In the edge of the evening a boat with two black fugitives came down the river. They had escaped from the rebels, but brought us very little useful intelligence regarding their numbers or position. Yesterday a black boy came in from the enemy's lines with large stories about their force, size of their guns, &c. The rebel general had made his men a speech, and they were to attack us yesterday morning. General Foster thinks the boy was sent in, and so has quartered him in the guard house. At all events, the rebels did not appear this morning. In fact they seem inclined to give us plenty of time, which, of course, we are improving to the best of our ability, by the erection of traverses, additional breastworks and forts. We have also placed upon the top of our earthworks three or four thicknesses of turf. The block-house where our company is stationed is on the extreme left of our line of defence, and is consequently most exposed to an attack from up the river, which is among the strong probabilities of this siege. Flat boats and steamers provided with guns and armor of cotton bales are reported above, and are expected to join in the attack when the land forces get ready, provided they escape certain formidable river obstructions intended for their benefit.

We are strongly posted, but are few in numbers. Our entire garrison, armed contrabands included, scarcely amounts to two thousand men. The gunboats have failed in silencing the rebel shore batteries, and we know not but the river is substantially blockaded. Of course we shall soon be short of provisions. Our chief ground of hope for release, in case the rebel attack is longer deferred, is in the arrival of forces from Newbern, or from Suffolk overland. General Foster was looking for aid from General [John A.] Dix [in Virginia] yesterday. Of course the aid did not arrive,— it never does.

We had a strong picket out again last night, but everything was remarkably quiet. Our incorrigible Jo says the pickets of the two forces were so near together that they distinctly heard each other eating hard tack! To-day the rebel pickets on the north side are reported to have disappeared, but this morning the rebels on the south side of the river are sending their Whitworth "cucumbers" into town in a very lively manner.[9]

A rebel deserter who came in a day or two ago reports that he was one of the squad that was unfortunately fired upon by one of our howitzers a few days ago, under the supposition that they were rebels. He also reports that the man whom one of our videttes saw suspended to an apple-tree was one of his companions who had been captured by a rebel cavalryman and summarily executed.

APRIL 9.

The rebel batteries kept pretty busy yesterday, but attracted little notice from the gunboats. Four new rebel batteries were discovered on this side [of] the river, about twelve hundred yards east of our most eastern blockhouse. They are intended to command our fort. Two of them are thought to contain one small gun each, the third, a twelve-pounder, and the fourth a siege gun. The enemy have one thirty-two-pounder on the other side of the river, but we doubtless outnumber them in heavy artillery. They will find Fort Washington a hard nut, and there are heavier pieces on board the gunboats than have yet disturbed the echoes hereabout. All Commodore [Richard T.] Renshaw asks is a land force to capture the rebel guns after he has dismounted them. Such a force we hope is not far distant. The music of their artillery is reported to have been heard yesterday and last night.

Yesterday we witnessed the affecting scene of a soldier's funeral at our blockhouse. The deceased was Isaac Powers, of Co. B, Mass. 27th, who met his death by falling down a flight of stairs in the blockhouse. At the close of the services, the deep boom of the rebel siege gun came across the water with thrilling effect. The peculiarity and danger of our situation were earnestly alluded to by Chaplain Woodworth, as an incentive to preparation for the great change which in the fortunes of war so soon might visit a large number of us.

This morning (and this is to be the rule during the present condition of affairs) we were called out for roll-call between three and four o'clock, and then stationed behind the breastworks until sunrise. We are living upon three-quarters rations, but thus far have kept hunger well at bay. Gen. Foster has taken possession of all provisions for sale in Washington, and says we can subsist on them thirty or forty days. We have despatched a few cattle, but the meat is poor stuff—lean and garlicy—barely fit to eat.

APRIL 10.

Our prospects are brightening. Last night two schooners from Newbern, loaded with ammunition and forage, passed the blockade, and arrived here safely. Those in charge of the vessels inform us that a large force of infantry is on the way by land from Newbern.

Contrabands who came in yesterday report the rebels confident of having us in their power, and as saying that they can keep back any reinforcements which may be sent to us.

The 44th Regiment has met with an irreparable loss in the death of its excellent surgeon, Dr. [Robert] Ware, who expired this morning, after a painful sickness of several days. His disease is supposed to have been the malarious fever peculiar to this locality, but it is suggested that death was hastened by the heavy artillery firing this morning incident to the opening of new rebel batteries on a hill east of the town. One week ago no event could have been more unexpected by us. With a frame compact, sinewy and nervous, Dr. Ware was the apparent embodiment of physical health. His, surely, we thought, was a constitution firm and elastic enough to withstand not only the effects of the climate but of professional labors made doubly severe by an assiduity and tenderness which had won the affection and the reverence of the whole regiment. But death, mindless of all human calculations, has ended the life and usefulness of Dr. Ware at a time which adds peculiar providential mystery to the event, inasmuch as the necessity of his skillful ministrations was perhaps never more imminent than at the moment of his death. This, however, is not the chief reason why we lament his death. We mourn the loss of the true, inestimable man, more than that of the able, experienced surgeon. Dr. Ware was the son of the venerable Dr. Robert Ware, of Boston.

For the last two mornings the rebel batteries to the east have performed lively reveilles. Fort Washington, in the centre of our outward line of entrenchments, was the object of their attention; but several shells have reached our extreme left, a piece of one striking close to the shanties of Company D's boys, bounding thence into the river. The fort replies to these sallies with excellent effect, and always has the last word, the rebels withdrawing. Thus far the number of our wounded is extremely small, and the gratifying fact is doubtless in a measure due to the traverses which intersect the outer breastwork, thereby preventing the unpleasant effects of a raking fire parallel with the entrenchments. Yesterday some of Company A's shelter tents were riddled while the boys were safe behind their traverse. Besides this defence, we are still more securely guarded against the rebel artillery from the east by bomb-proofs on the western side of the traverses. We found it practicable to avail ourselves of their protection this morning, but we enlivened the chilly gloom of the retreat by singing various choice arias from, Il Recruitio.

Between the building and turfing of earthworks, bomb-proofs, standing guard and doing nightly picket duty, we are kept pretty hard at work, and are beginning to feel the combined effects of the hard knocks and poor rations. We have considerable use for lumber, and Grist's cotton mill and other out-buildings are levied upon accordingly. Having secured the boards and joists, we transport them to the fortifications upon the wheels of Grist's old family carriage. Since this man left town, renewed suspicions of thorough treachery have taken possession of the soldiers, and the Grist mansion itself would hardly be safe if the red hospital flag did not wave over it.

This morning the music of a rebel band floated to our ears from over the river. This afternoon we have had the thorough bass of their big guns on the same side, sending bomb-shells into town. And no reinforcements yet! We are very anxious to see them, but not greatly surprised at their non-arrival, considering the lions they will find in their way, in the shape of unbridged streams, fallen trees, and rebel forts and rifle-pits.

Attached to some of the oblong shells which were sent into town this morning, were some of the Shenckl percussion fuses, bearing the mark of George H. Fox & Co., of Boston, manufacturers. Perhaps the gentlemen of this firm will be interested in the fact. Boston boys think it a little funny to meet such specimens of home manufacture in North Carolina.

A night or two ago our pickets on the Jamesville road got beyond the outposts of the enemy, and had an unexpected rencounter with the rebel pickets. The interview was quite cordial, but our boys were assured that the rebels had Washington in a vice. Many inside are of the same opinion, but of course this depends upon the success we may have in getting reinforcements through.

APRIL 13.

Night before last it was reported that the rebels were crossing the river above and below us, on flat-boats, with a view of strengthening themselves on the south side, to meet our reinforcements from Newbern. We also have rumors of fights on the Newbern road.

APRIL 14.

Last night steamers from below with reinforcements of men and provisions ran by the rebel batteries under a hot fire, and arrived safely at Washington. Our garrison is now strong, and our friends need have no fears concerning us. We are in the receipt of letters and papers to the 3d. inst.

It is said that the long delay in sending us reinforcements was caused by their repulse by the rebels on the Newbern road. But of this matter I can only give you rumors.[10] You can imagine that the loyal part of Little Washington is jubilant to-day.

*   *   *

Washington, N.C.,

APRIL 16, 1863.

My diary of the siege of Washington, forwarded to you by a steamer which left on the 14th, closed on the 13th, when I announced the gratifying intelligence of the arrival of reinforcements. Yesterday morning General Foster departed for Newbern, leaving behind the following general order:

Headquarters 18th Army Corps,
Washington, N.C., April 14th, 1863.

The Commanding General announces to the garrison of this town that he is about to leave for a brief space of time the gallant soldiers and sailors of this garrison. Brigadier General [Edward E.] Potter will remain in command, and in him the Commanding General has the most perfect confidence as a brave and able soldier. The command of the naval forces remains unchanged; therefore that arm of the service will be as effective and perfect as heretofore. The Commanding General leaves temporarily, and for the purpose of putting himself at the head of a relieving force. Having raised the siege, he expects soon to return; but before leaving he must express to the naval force here, and to the soldiers under his command, the 27th and 44th Massachusetts Regiments, detachments of the 3d New York Cavalry and 1st North Carolina Volunteers, his thanks for and admiration of the untiring zeal, noble emulation and excellent courage which have distinguished them during the sixteen days of the enemy's attack on this post; and he feels confident that the display of those qualities under General Potter will hold the place till the siege be raised.

J. G. Foster,
Gen. Commanding 18th Army Corps.

Regimental glorification is so prevalent a weakness on the part of newspaper correspondents in the army, that I am almost ashamed to state a fact which I know will be pleasing to our friends at home. I allude to a marked unofficial compliment from General Foster, who observed to Colonel Lee that the 44th regiment has performed more service than any other nine months' regiment in his department, and probably more than any other nine months' regiment in the field; that the conduct of the regiment had been in every respect spirited, honorable and gratifying to him. I offer this as a most thorough refutation of the villainous libels which the low enmity of a few men in the other Massachusetts regiments have dictated and set afloat.

The air is full of rumors discreditable to the generalship and bravery of General Spinola, who was last week sent from Newbern to relieve this garrison, in which attempt, it is reported, he miserably failed, and then fell back without a sufficient cause. If he has not done his duty, General Foster will be the last man to excuse the omission. He has chafed like a caged lion during the siege, and is said to have gone away mad as a March hare. The rebels did not omit the customary salute when his steamer passed down the river, and it is thought one or more cannon balls went through the upper works of the vessel. At the same time the rebel batteries to the east of the town played upon us in a lively manner, and sent us into our bomb-proofs upon the double-quick. The rebels amused themselves in the same manner on the previous morning, about the time the band was giving expression to our joy at receiving reinforcements, and in fact this has been the order of the day for a long time. But it has been no boys' play. Shot and shell have rained all along our line. Several of our shelter tents have been cut to pieces by them. I could recount scores of "miraculous escapes." Our bomb-proofs have probably been the means of saving many lives. It certainly seems scarcely short of Providential interposition that a bombardment extending over sixteen days has not resulted in the loss of a single life or limb on our side.

This morning five deserters have come in and report the rebels falling back on Greenville, [North Carolina]. The indications confirm the report.

Cavalry and infantry scouts find their breastworks this side of the river abandoned, and the rebs have not fired a gun to-day on either side. A thunder tempest raged last night, and it is highly probable that they skedaddled under the protection which the noise of the elements afforded them. Finding the blockade ineffective, they despaired of starving us out, and so have retired with great loss—of ammunition. In this respect it has been a very expensive siege to them; and it is believed that their loss in lives has not been inconsiderable. They have found Little Washington, under the engineering of General Foster, a hard nut to crack, and will scarce try the experiment again.

P.M. Our gunboats hammered away at the positions lately held by the rebels on the south side of the river, until being satisfied that they were no longer there, boats were sent to reconnoitre about Rodman's Point. It happened that a few of the enemy, probably their rear guard, were still on the ground. They rose and fired on our boats with fatal effect. An engineer of the gunboat Ceres was killed. Frank Tripp, of Company E, 43d regiment, in another boat, was very severely wounded. The boats then withdrew.

This morning our scouts visited the scene of the principal rebel bivouac this side [of] the river, and came to the conclusion that about two thousand men had encamped there.

Towards night the gunboats Hunchback, Southfield and two or three others, which during the siege had been hanging ten miles below, came up in range of Rodman's Point, and commenced shelling the woods with great vigor. The same amount of firing in the same places yesterday or day before would have placed the rebels in great danger of their limbs and lives; but before opening his fire the magnanimous commander of the down river fleet waited until our erring brethren had got beyond the reach of the Hunchback's hundred pounders, and then blazed away, to the mingled admiration and terror of the contraband population of Washington and vicinity. I am informed that the timely arrival of the Rhode Island 5th, which gallantly ran the blockade on the night of the 13th, was solely due to the energetic determination of Colonel [Henry T.] Sisson, in opposition to the naval authorities down the river. In other respects a nightmare retardation has seemed to characterize all attempts to relieve this garrison.

* * *

Hill's Point, 8 Miles below Washington, N.C., South Side of Sound,

APRIL 17, 1863.

Companies C, D, and I were ordered on board the gunboat Eagle last evening, where we slept. This morning we landed in small boats at this place. It was the strongest point of the rebel blockade. Behind the earthworks, which were mostly erected at an early day in the rebellion, are a plenty of bomb-proofs. The natural defences of the place are remarkable for this flat vicinity. Behind the earthworks is a pleasant piece of tableland, which we now occupy. Between the shore and the woods is a rebel rifle-pit. This forenoon we skirmished out a mile or so, encountering an old rebel camp and the one the rebels have recently occupied. We picked up one butternut [Confederate] gentleman with a carpet bag containing a rebel uniform, and the picture of a rebel officer. Butternut said he picked up the carpet bag in the woods as he was going home from [the] mill. He said the rebs were robbing the population of their provisions and had nearly cleaned him out. There was a "right smart" of rebs here, but they left in a hurry night before last. Three companies of the 43d, C, D, and H, landed here from schooners about noon. They had been lying below the blockade for a week or so, with the other companies of their regiment, who had been suddenly called back to Newbern. The 43d formed part of Spinola's late expedition, and the boys of that regiment are emphatic in their denunciation of the conduct of the General in retreating without, as they say, sufficient cause. Their march back, after getting within ten miles of Newbern [Washington?], was of the most forced and exhausting description. The affair will probably be investigated by a court martial.

The excellent sketch of our situation and defences at Washington, which accompanies this letter, was drawn by George W. Hight, of Company D.[11] I have no doubt you will take pleasure in showing it to any friend of the 44th regiment who may call for that purpose.

APRIL 18, 1863.

The detachment of the 44th Regiment stationed at this point [Hill's Point] are quite delighted with their situation. We have seen nothing so pleasant in North Carolina. The Tar river here widens into Pamlico Sound, and from our position on this bluff or table land, it spreads out before us like a beautiful lake in the woods. This morning, one of the loveliest of Spring, the air is fragrant with pines and flowers, and melodious with the songs of birds. The field is dotted with fruit trees in bloom. Yesterday we found the woods spangled with jasmine, violets, box and dog-wood, and our skirmishers with their hands full of flowers looked more like a Maying party than soldiers expecting a foe in every bush.[12] A rebel soldier lies buried beneath a branching cedar close to our bivouac, the living and the dead sleeping together. Upon the headboard of the latter we read "Henry Davenport, 52d North Carolina Regiment." His resting place was selected with true refinement of taste.

APRIL 20.

From our picket post yesterday we caught the sound of wild cheering, which we soon learned was given to the advance of our army from Newbern, headed by General Foster. To-day we learn that three of our brigades are in Washington, another in the vicinity of Kinston, and another between here and Newbern. Feint movements are perhaps involved in this disposition of troops, but we have no idea of what General Foster is about. He is reinforced by the return of part of his troops from the Department of the South, including the Massachusetts 23d and the New Jersey 9th. The Massachusetts 24th and the Connecticut 10th are still with General [David] Hunter.[13]

We are in receipt to-day of letters from the North, containing newspaper slips devoted to late affairs in this vicinity. The letter of a correspondent at Newbern, which the Boston Journal accepts as "the clearest account of affairs at Washington and Newbern," is a complete tissue of errors, of a character so serious that the regiment has been excited to indignation by their unfortunate publicity.

The statement that Companies A and D went outside the earthworks and had their retreat cut off, contains two errors. Company D did not go out at all until after the blockade was raised, and the retreat of Company A was not cut off. The "cutting their way through with the loss of sixteen" is also a pure fiction, as is the announcement of the death of Orderly Sergeant [Thomas S.] Edmands. Our total loss in the affair alluded to was three wounded, who were taken prisoners. Orderly Sergeant Edmands was not one of these, but the careless statement of his death has doubtless plunged a circle of friends into mourning as sorrowful and deep, for a time, as the event itself could produce. Then who shall undertake to estimate the anxiety and torture of suspense in the minds of the friends of Companies A and D before they shall find out the falsity of the story of "sixteen killed?" Our laws are defective in their want of penalties for such outrageous sins against the tenderest and sacredest feelings of nature as those perpetrated by a class of irresponsible correspondents, who seize upon and circulate rumors for facts, and who mutilate the king's English and human feelings with about equal facility and *sang froid.*

* * *

In Tow of Steamer Thomas Collyer,

WEDNESDAY, APRIL 23, 1863.

Having contributed to the salvation of Little Washington, we are now on our way back to the "home camp" at Newbern, leaving Hill's Point garrisoned by a portion of the 43d, and Washington by several New York and Pennsylvania regiments, together with the Massachusetts 27th and part of the 43d. Accompanying us on our way back to Newbern are five companies of the Rhode Island 5th, and two companies of the Massachusetts 46th. We have been absent from Newbern over five weeks, and now the near prospect of getting into our barracks again has elated every heart. Lots of boxes for us have accumulated in our absence, and our anxiety to be at them is quite intense. We have, to tell the truth, a harrowing suspicion that the invalid guard, actuated by an unselfish purpose to keep them from spoiling, will save us the trouble not only of opening the boxes but of eating the contents. Heaven forbid, however! In our present half-famished condition this is no trifling thought.

CHAPTER 8

Provost Duty

Newbern, N.C.

APRIL 24.

Here we are at old Newbern again, but not at "home," as we fondly call our old barracks while absent on expeditions. We found the New Jersey 9th in our old quarters, so we betook ourselves to the barracks of our old and beloved neighbors, the Conn. 10th. But we are to stay here only a short time. Saturday we are going down into the city to do provost-guard duty, and shall probably continue in that capacity the remainder of our term of service. We shall there be quartered in houses, and, except in extreme cases, be excused from participating in expeditions. This will please those of our timorous friends who, when we left home, gravely and affectionately admonished us not to get shot. There is now, dear friends, a right smart chance for us to escape rebel bullets, "except," as Sparrowgrass once remarked, "in case of invasion."

To-day we were formally installed as provost-guard of Newbern, thereby relieving the 45th regiment, which has for a considerable time been acting in the same capacity. The 45th received us with all the honors, and we stood at present arms as they marched past us in going out of the city. Each regiment bore its regimental colors and was headed by its band.

Our company (D) are put in possession of a commodious wooden mansion and its out-buildings on Pollock street, lately occupied by Co. A, of the 45th. We found the rooms in neat condition, and decorated with wreaths and bouquets of flowers, accompanied by the pleasant salutatory words, "WELCOME 44," several times inscribed on the walls. The "Jolly Five" have the thanks of "Corporal," and his mess for their part in a greeting so graceful on one side and so grateful to the other.

The 54th regiment has made another draft upon the 44th for officers, Charles E. Tucker, Co. E, Williard Howard and Henry W. Littlefield, of Co. D, having just received their commissions as lieutenants in the former.[1] They will leave for Boston to-morrow.

I learn that the officers of our regiment have decided to present to the Fifth Regiment of Rhode Island a stand of colors as a slight acknowledgment of the gallantry of that regiment in running the rebel blockade and coming to our relief at Washington. The Mass. 27th, with whom we were blockaded, is now in Newbern.

To-day the regiment have attended the obsequies of our late lamented and beloved Surgeon, Dr. Ware, to whose unexpected death we are none of us quite reconciled. His remains will be carried to Boston by the steamer Ellen S. Terry, which leaves Newbern to-day.

This letter is carried to Boston by H. P. Tuttle, late of the Cambridge Observatory, who has just been discharged from the 44th regiment on account of having received a commission as Assistant Paymaster in the Navy.

Our life as provost guard at Newbern is too uneventful to call for much letter writing. We have been joined by companies B and F, who have been a long while on picket, and we are now a regiment of policemen. The rank and file are on guard almost every other day, and the duty is found at once severe, irksome, and often abhorrent. I am rather glad that our present reputation as policemen is not to be the measure of our characters as soldiers. I am loath to confess that we were getting to be beloved by the tough ones of the old regiments, who, since pay-day, which occurred recently, found three dollars a bottle for whisky no bar to indulgence in that popular stimulant, and who have an acquired loathing of the guard-house. However, we are becoming very exemplary policemen, if I may judge from the curses (both loud and deep) which are showered upon the devoted heads of the 44th regiment, and nine months' men generally.

Newbern is looking very attractive, The gardens are still rich with roses of every hue. I wish the paper May-flower girls of Boston could be turned amongst them for a day.

We have small time or opportunity for amusement, although I have no doubt that the shoulder straps [officers] find provost-guard life extremely bully, setting aside some of the severe duties which belong to them as moral conservators. They are treated to concerts, attend private music parties, and regale themselves with ice water,—very good in this latitude at this season. The privates are solicited to produce another opera; and an entertainment of that character, founded upon the siege of Washington, together with a regimental concert, a dramatic performance, and a *bal masque,* is upon the tapis.

Weddings, white and colored, are just now the subject of gossip. One of our own corporals has been and gone and done it, and one of the pretty natives of Newbern is now Mrs. Lawrence. Last night some of our boys assisted at a darkey wedding, putting the happy pair to bed in true traditional style.

Our nights are rendered musical by the plaintive choral hymnings of devotional negroes in every direction, alone and in groups. From their open cabins come the mingled voices of men wrestling painfully and agonizingly with the spirit, and those uttering the ecstatic notes of the redeemed.

* * *

Newbern, N.C.,

MAY 16, 1863.

We are in a state of stagnation. We have not been so unhappy since the date of our enlistment as we have since we entered upon the police business at Newbern. We have almost forgotten the toil and misery of long marches and sieges, and revert with something like regret to the days of active campaigning. I have no doubt that many of us will voluntarily return to the army should the state of the country call for more service at our hands. We rejoice that we have had a hand in this glorious contest for the integrity of our country. No sacrifice or hardship we have endured balances the gratification of having done our country some service, however small or humble that service may have been. If we had but one word of advice to give the young men of our acquaintance, it would be to enlist voluntarily while a chance remains to identify yourselves in a glorious warfare which is evidently drawing to such a termination as every patriot must pray and fight for. Do not stand back because you think the danger is past. We may safely calculate that much work remains to be done. The serpent of secession is only scotched, not killed. The clouds may yet again lower over us, and every strong arm may be needed to sweep them away.

How well the magnificent strategy and the more magnificent fighting of our New England General comports with his clear, ringing testimony before the Committee on the Conduct of the War![2]

How stands McClellan presidential stock at the North? Who will heal up the wounds of the copperheads? Nothing will keep them from despair but the injudicious arrest and imprisonment of blatant politicians who hunger and thirst after martyrdom, and who do not know that their advocacy of a cause is its most effective condemnation.

MAY 18.

A "trance medium" by the name of James Richardson, of Athol, in Co. B, 27th regiment, assures the members of his regiment that they will be discharged from the service in less than a year from this time, and that the war will be brought to a close before that time. His associates, although professing to have no faith in asserted revelations of this kind, are forced to confess that Richardson has proved to be a true prophet in several important instances. He foretold the battles of Roanoke and Newbern, and with so many of their particulars as to prove his possession of a power altogether unexplainable. He foretold the siege of Washington by stating that the 27th regiment would take part in a long but not very bloody battle, and that a certain man would be killed. Following this came the seventeen days' siege, and the death of the man alluded to. After this battle he said the regiment would soon remove to another place in transports. That has also happened. From that place, in two or four months, they were to embark in transports for the North.

Orderly Sergeant [Horace S.] Stebbins of Co. F has been commissioned as second lieutenant in place of Lieut. [Alfred F.] Hartwell, now a captain in the 54th. Lieut. Stebbins is a much esteemed officer, capable and prompt, without being a tyrant or a martinet.

Private [Henry F.] Melville, of Co. A, died on Friday of inflammation of the bowels. Since our return from Washington, most of the regiment have been much troubled with diarrhea, which, however, is now subsiding. The average health of the regiment is good. Dr. [Theodore W.] Fisher, assistant surgeon with the late Dr. Ware, is now surgeon of the regiment. He is a man of much professional skill and faithfulness. His assistant, Dr. [Daniel] McPhee, is winning golden opinions for the same qualities, united with great complaisance to everybody but "niggers." He was with the English army during the Sepoy rebellion.[3]

At dress parade this evening an order, suitably acknowledging the generous gift of $500 at the hands of Mr. Gilmore, for the benefit of the 44th regiment, was read.

* * *

Newbern, N.C.,

MAY 23, 1863.

The Newbern markets are points of some interest. What native products are offered for sale here are chiefly brought in small sail vessels from up and down the river, their place of rendezvous being at the foot of Pollock street. Due notice of the arrival of produce being given at the office of the Provost-Marshal, the sale commences, under such restriction as this functionary may have been pleased to prescribe. If the cargo is of eggs, the hospitals and certain functionaries must first be provided for. After this, private soldiers and negroes may be allowed to buy one or two dozens each. The scenes about these market boats are sometimes quite animated and interesting. This morning a boat lay at the wharf with eggs, sweet potatoes and green peas. The butternut [Southern] skipper and his son were beset in a very confusing manner. First went the green peas, half grown, at fifty cents a peck. Then the eggs at twenty-five cents a dozen. Anxious but patient darkeys of both sexes, ancient and lean Carolinians of the white "persuasion" and doubtful loyalty, eyed the sweet potatoes and bided their doubtful chances.

The only cheap thing in Newbern is fish—drum, sheepshead, trout, herring, &c., caught down the sound. Trout enough for a family dinner can be bought for twenty-five cents. It is very good, and the staple article of food at the restaurants.

A few farmers who were so fortunate as not to live on the line of our expeditionary raids, send in a little honey. Strawberries, also, are occasionally received.

Recruiting for the African brigade is progressing lively and enthusiastically. Quite a recruiting fever has seized the freedmen of Newbern. Recruiting offices will soon be opened at Washington and Plymouth. Four thousand colored soldiers are counted upon in this department. There is likely to be one item of compensation to the Government for holding these posts upon the enemy's soil. It is, indeed, due to the freedmen that we provide these harbors of refuge for those who escape from the rebel lines. There is, perhaps, not a slave in North Carolina who does not know that he may find freedom in Newbern, and thus Newbern may be the Mecca of a thousand noble aspirations. Leave Newbern to the rebels and hope would die out altogether in many a poor trembling heart. Thank God that the noble inspiration of human liberty is with us in this war. It helps us to abide temporary disaster, and is our pledge of final success. But we shall find a path stony and blood-moistened so long as we fail to have mercy and deal justly with the unoffending people who are the innocent cause of this war.

The regimental band of the 44th has grown into a fine institution under the combined labors of our chief musician, Mr. [George L.] Babcock, and the leader, Mr. H. H. Ingraham. Their repertory of music is large and fine and played with expression. Much of it was arranged by A. W. Ingraham, a brother of the leader, who has recently visited us. A third brother, also a member of the band, died in [the] hospital last winter. Very much is due to this musical trio, and perhaps not less to the fine orchestral taste of Mr. Babcock, for the striking proficiency attained by the band. Considering the excellent moral effect of good music in camp, we can hardly overestimate the thoughtful generosity of those friends who provided us with musical instruments. If "sounds of home" by them invoked have kept a single heart from going astray, the gift could not have been amiss.

Two hundred rebel prisoners, including a Colonel and several line officers, have just been captured near Kinston, by a brigade under command of Col. [J. Richter] Jones, of the Pennsylvania 58th. Beside the 58th, the Mass. 5th and 27th took part in the expedition. We had a few men wounded. The rebels suffered much more.[4]

* * *

Newbern, N.C.,

Your correspondent with the Eighteenth Army Corps proposes to deliver a series of "lectures upon the war" after he shall have returned to Boston. The topics to be embraced in the proposed series will include not only operations in the Department of North Carolina, but in those of the South and Gulf, if not in Virginia and the Southwest, his observations having convinced him that it is by no means necessary to see a battle to describe it with all desirable particularity and enthusimoosy [sic]. Tickets will be placed at one dollar. Your correspondent undertakes this disinterested and benevolent enterprise in consequence of the great dearth of information with reference to the war; but preliminary to his appearance he wishes to engage the services of the experienced dramatic editor of the Boston Herald for a proper introduction in his new capacity to the Athenian world. He will understand the importance of a suitable *invitation,* and will please allow your correspondent to refer him to a formula among the advertisements in Boston papers of a late date. To the document, modelled according to this suggestion, he will then secure the autographs of Honorable Edward Everett, Honorable Robert C. Winthrop,[5] *et id omnes genus,* by means of which those eminently respectable gentlemen will be made to express the deep interest with which they have perused the letters of "Corporal" in the Boston Herald, and their burning anxiety to hear him continue his elucidation of such noble theme as bal masques, hard tack, camp opera, salt horse, &c., &c. The dramatic editor, after reference to another formula among the advertisements of late Boston papers, will then indite [compose] a noble reply to the invitation, expressing the willingness of "Corporal" to give a public recital of his experience with hard tack, musty rice and shrivelled beans, during the period that he stood up for his country. He may mention June 17th as the time, and Faneuil Hall [Boston] as the place. This "Interesting Correspondence" must then be published in all the Boston papers, free, if possible, but if not possible, regardless of expense. It is not expected that Faneuil Hall will contain the crowd which will be attracted to its portals; but the public, being a capricious, theatre-going monster, may not turn out as anticipated, so, Mr. Dramatic Editor, I charge you to secure, by a bribe, the attendance of a reporter from each Boston paper, so that the aforesaid monster shall not go unlightened by the oral disquisitions of your correspondent.[6]

The fly-statistics of your Port Royal [South Carolina] correspondent must not lead your readers to suppose that the Department of the South enjoys a monopoly of this interesting insect. I allude to common house flies. Fleas and musquitoes [*sic*] do not greatly abound at Newbern, but house flies swarm like the locusts of Egypt. The wood ticks of Hill's Point, which adhered to the cuticle with a death-grasp, deserved a paragraph, but the house flies of Newbern are even a greater nuisance. The printer will not fail to notice the peculiar manner in which they have punctuated this sheet of manuscript. Their tracks are visible upon every object which they can touch—upon our plates, dippers, knives, forks, bread. They attack us with desperation at meal times, and if we have anything better than usual they are sure to find it out, and rally upon the sweet point, so that while we convey the food to our mouth with one hand, we are forced to fight flies with the other. "Tempus fugit," commences a letter of your Newbern correspondent, "Tiger." "Fly time—very appropriate," parenthetically remarked the free translator Frederick, as he read and described curves in the air.

Among recent visitors here have been Hon. Mr. Comins and wife, of Roxbury. General [Edward A.] Wild and staff, of the African brigade, in process of formation, are here.

* * *

Newbern, N.C.,

The recent dash by one of our brigades near Kinston, which resulted in the capture of about two hundred rebel soldiers, was followed by an angry spite on the part of the rebels in that direction, who gave our pickets some trouble, and who, by the agency of a sharpshooter, succeeded in killing Colonel Jones, of the Penn. 58th—one of the most brave officers and excellent men in the service; one of the [Andrew] Jackson type of soldiers, fighting heart and hand, and praying also for the success of the Union cause. We hate to lose such men. We have none such to spare. We wonder that a good cause is bereft of such auxiliaries, and are perhaps too slow to learn the lesson that individual men are of little account in eliminating the grand designs of Providence. We need to be cured of hero-worship. It has been one of the banes interfering with the due progress of the war. We may safely put faith in men collectively, and in the principles which prevade [*sic*] the masses of the North, but never in any single man or set of men.

Company F, Captain Storrow has gone to Fortress Monroe, having in charge a lot of rebel prisoners. We expect the company will come back to Newbern and accompany the regiment home.

Another levy has been made upon us for officers in regiments of colored men. Privates W. D. Crane of Company D, [Frank] Goodwin, [George W.] Woodward, and Sergeant [George M.] Weld, of Company F, are among those who propose leaving Newbern for Boston to-day to take commissions as line officers in one or more of these regiments.

Some of the more festive of the line officers in this department have recently assisted at a variegated affair called a nigger ball, which transpired at the house of Black Lovinia, one of the Skittletop sisterhood. Not the least interested and observant spectators of this *recherche* affair were one or two sentinels in the vicinity, who tell curious stories of the carryings-on. The assemblage occupied two stories of the building, the lower rooms being partly devoted to dancing; but some of the movements were not recognized in any of the modern schottisches, waltzes, or polka-redowas.

It was a marbled crowd, the upper stratum being described as yellow and white, and the lower one pure black and white. So, with strange indifference to the articles of war, say those prying fellows, the nocturnal sentinels.

The rebel guerrillas, who are always prowling around Newbern, succeeded recently in catching a couple of schooners becalmed down the river, and burned them, to the water's edge.

Our convalescents are sent down to Beaufort and Morehead City for the benefit to be derived from sea air. The principal hospital was formerly a large hotel. It stands upon piles, and the tides flow beneath it. The patients ride in sail boats, eat strawberries, and disport with the fair secesh of Beaufort, who are quite an improvement upon the tallow-faced damsels of the interior.

* * *

Newbern, N.C.,
MAY 29, 1863.

As our nine months' service draws to its close, time drags its slow length along in the most irritating manner possible. This police life would soon demoralize, if it did not kill us quite. We have already lost not a little of our former excellency in drill, and we have dubious anticipations as to the figure we shall cut on Boston Common.

If we arrive in Boston before the expiration of our term of service, there is a probability of our spending a few days in camp at Readville, where we hope to recover our military stamina, and where we shall be at home to our old friends of blessed memory.

In a recent letter containing a reference to the band, I said that we had been visited by A. W. Ingraham, to whose skillful arrangement of music, much of the excellency of the band was due. Mr. Ingraham has since assumed the leadership, and his splendid bugle playing is now a marked and attractive feature of the music at serenades and dress parades.

On the 27th our regiment being formally mustered agreeable to an order from headquarters, we were addressed by General Foster and solicited to join the new heavy artillery regiment. The General was heartily cheered, but I think very few of the boys will care to re-enlist until they have seen Massachusetts once more, although furloughs and other inducements are tendered. The artillery branch of the service, the Department of North Carolina, and General Foster are all to the liking of our regiment, and many of its members are likely to return here.

The 27th was General Foster's birthday. In the evening his residence was brilliantly lighted and crowded with guests. Music, gaiety and splendid hospitality graced the occasion—contrasting strangely with the impressive ceremonials of the preceding day attending the removal of the remains of Colonel Jones to the steamer.

Captain [William V.] Smith, of Company H, Lieutenants [James E.] Newell, of Company E, and [Frederic] Odiorne, of Company G, Orderly Sergeant [Edward P.] White, of Company E, Orderly Sergeant [Charles A.] Cunningham, of Company C, and private [Joseph H.] Curtis, of Company F, are to take commissions in a new regiment of heavy artillery recruiting for this garrison, and to be under the command of Major [Jones] Frankle, of the Massachusetts 17th regiment, as Colonel.

Orderly Sergeant [John L.] Mulliken, of Company H, has been elected Second Lieutenant, in place of Lieutenant [Albert R.] Howe, promoted to be First Lieutenant, in place of Lieutenant [Edward C.] Johnson, appointed Adjutant, in place of Lieutenant [Wallace] Hinkley, who is to be Adjutant of the artillery regiment. Since writing the above, I learn that a number of our regiment, as well as a number in the 43d and 45th, have decided to join as privates.

* * *

Newbern, N.C.,

By a blunder of the printer, I was made in a recent letter to allude to Lieut. [Alfred S.] Hartwell, of the Mass. 55th, as a former second lieutenant of Co. F. He was first lieutenant of that company, and much distinguished as a disciplinarian, as well as for his moral qualities.

Intelligence has just been received here of the death in a rebel hospital of Orderly Sergeant [David K.] Hobart, of Co. G, who was wounded and captured near Washington, March 30, at the commencement of the siege of that place. This intelligence comes by way of Washington, D.C., through official sources. Nothing is known here of the fate of private [John] Leonard, who was severely wounded and captured at the same time.

Some objection is made to the use of the word "police," as descriptive of our duties in Newbern. I have used it in the civil and not in the military sense of the word. Police duty, in a military sense, is the duty of cleaning camp. As provost-guard of Newbern, our duty is to "clean out" disreputable places, to see that soldiers in town are not absent from their regiments without leave, and to attend to moral publicans generally.

The negroes here honor the Hibernian custom of "waking" their dead. On occasions of this sort, they sometimes render night so hideous by their songs and shoutings that the guard is attracted to the scene of their spiritual orgies, to enforce order. At midnight, the revellers solemnly refresh themselves with coffee, and then resume their howling, reciting and chanting simple hymns, line by line.

Several transports are lying here and at Morehead, in one of which a cavalry company arrived on the 29th ult. On the same day, Co. F returned from Fortress Monroe, whither they had been sent to guard prisoners sent from Newbern. Another transport arrived yesterday with more cavalry.

Lieuts. [James W.] Briggs and [Benjamin F.] Field, detached from the regiment some months ago to serve on the signal corps in the Department of the South, have returned to Newbern, and will go home with the regiment. Detailed men are ordered to report to their companies on or before the 8th, about the time we are expected to leave for home. It is said all our sick will be taken with us. Even the most protracted cases of "convalescence" at Beaufort will hardly forego the glory of "marching up State street," the only avenue to Boston by which a returning regiment could possibly get into the city. Will the great army of quidnuncs, the men with green spectacles, umbrellas and towering shirt collars, coatless quill-drivers, the breechless admirers of brass bands, and the floating population generally take the hint? What avails going to the war if there can be no State street finale with the customary remarks of the reporters so nicely adjusted to the merits of each individual corps? How inscrutable are the judgments of reporters until their impressions come to light in good fair type, when we find that the last regiment, like all the preceding ones, "looked finely and marched like veterans!" Of course we shall be proud to be noticed; and if the great army of sight-seers, (without whom "marching up State street" would be as apples of Sodom,) shall really enjoy the coming novelty of a regiment marching up State street, will voluntarily swell the number of those soon to march *down* street, we shall feel more than paid for having afforded them a sensation, at the expense of our blushing modesty.

CHAPTER 9

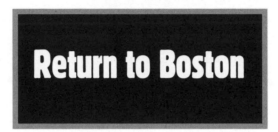

Return to Boston

JUNE 6, 1863.

At this writing (half past one o'clock P.M.) the 44th regiment, pleasantly quartered on board the transport steamers "Guide" and "George Peabody," is steaming out of Beaufort (N.C.) harbor, bound for dear old Boston. Just as the train of open cars which bore us from Newbern to Morehead City this morning was getting under way, the clouds opened with rain as though determined to treat us with a parting baptism, as well as the introductory one by which we were drenched through and through on our way from Morehead City to Newbern last October. But in this respect we were agreeably disappointed. It rained but little, and the sunbeams came through so many vapory clouds that the weather was delightful. Nine months' absence from the sea coast had sharpened an old love for ocean breezes; and as we neared Morehead, the sweet smells of the beach mingled with the refreshing coolness coming

"From where old Triton blows his wreathed horn,"[1]

were inhaled with delight and gratitude.

The right wing of our regiment is on board the Guide. The right wing includes companies A, G, H, K, and E. The Colonel, Lieut.-Colonel, and Major, the regimental band, the surgeon, and the sick, are also on board the Guide.

The left wing is upon the George Peabody. We consist of companies F, B, D, C, and I, under command of senior Captain Storrow.

Being the slower boat, we have the start. The weather continues delightful; the sea is azure: and, as we turn our prow northward, satisfaction and joyful anticipations hover over us beautiful as birds of paradise.

I believe we carry with us from the department of North Carolina the cordial good will of Gen. Foster. That this sentiment is fully reciprocated by our regiment the enthusiasm in its ranks always excited by the presence of the General is abundant proof. He honored the occasion of our departure by coming out to the depot with his full staff. He was greeted with a storm of cheers, which he and staff heartily returned. Last night he received our officers at his residence in a very complimentary manner. In the meantime the quarters of several of the companies were illuminated, the boys exchanged visits in a very unceremonious and jubilant manner, and cheered everybody and everything without regard to sex or condition. So passed the eve of our departure from Newbern. This morning the Mass. 3d regiment, Captain [Silas P.] Richmond, honored us by escorting the 44th to the depot.

We are succeeded as provost guard by the Mass. 27th, one of the noblest bodies of men in the service.

JUNE 7, 1863.

We had heavy showers and a high wind last night. Many of the deck sleepers were driven below. Those who remained found their clothes and blankets saturated with water this morning. Our guns, late the pride of the regiment, were covered with rust. A stiff wind was blowing from the northwest, and the unsteady motion of the boat was beginning to have the customary effect on landsmen. We turned out this morning a dismal-looking set; but, as the day advanced, we presently discovered blue sky enough to make a pair of breeches for a Dutchman, and then we knew we were safe, according to the best marine logic.[2] Still later the sun struggled into view, cheering our hearts and drying out blankets at the same time. Contrary to the general impression, I find that there was but little sea-sickness last night. It was something else,—sourness of the stomach, sickness of the stomach, headache, &c., but the symptoms were wonderfully uniform.

On board the George Peabody, with our left wing, are about one hundred men from the 46th, 43d, 8th, and other Massachusetts nine months regiment, going home on a furlough, having enlisted in Col. Frankle's regiment of heavy artillery, at Newbern.

JUNE 9.

The interim indicated by my last two dates was covered by indisposition—not sea-sickness, of course, but something mightily like it in all its external indications. I may here mention that we have had a pretty rough trip, steaming for most of the time directly against a northeaster. As a natural result, thirteen were in the hospital last night, and the venerable captain of the Peabody was forced to retire to his cabin and solemnly take an observation through the skylight every thirty minutes.

We have been cheered by one reminiscence of camp life, to wit, roll-call. The homeward-bound citizen soldiery, thinking routine about played out, answered *en masse* for every name as it was called, and found it impossible, in consequence of the roughness of the sea, to keep from tumbling over each other, to the great detriment of the proper company rectilinear. Roll-call on shipboard was thenceforward dispensed with as impracticable, if not impossible. It was with no small satisfaction that our eyes opened this morning to find the Peabody making its way up Vineyard Sound, between beautiful, bold, green shores dotted with villages and more scattered white cottages, eloquent of thrift and industry which cannot live with slavery and rebellion.

7 O'CLOCK, P.M.

We were streaming up in the track of a golden sunset this evening toward dear old Boston, when our progress was arrested by a terrible being on a tug-boat, who first demanded the name of our regiment, and then ordered us to haul to. We obeyed. We then inquired of the terrible being, who wore two rows of brass buttons, if our escort, the Guide, had arrived? "Who is the officer in command?" again demanded the being, not choosing to hear the question. He was informed. The being then boarded us, waving us from before him with both hands. He retired to the cabin for a conference, and presently emerged therefrom, but what is to come of all this we can only conjecture with fear and trembling. We may have to wait on board for the Guide, which we now for the first time are apprised, is behind us, but there is a talk of putting us into Fort Independence. Of one thing, however, we are sure: We have seen Major-Generals and even a Major-General of an Army Corps, but General Foster, in all his glory, can hold no candle to the terrible being who came upon us from the tug.

THE WELCOME HOME

The Boston Herald, of June 10th, gives the following account of the welcome home extended to the 44th Regiment:

THE RECEPTION OF THE FORTY-FOURTH REGIMENT.

As was anticipated, the transport steamer Guide, with the right wing of the 44th regiment, arrived here about 6 o'clock this morning, and steamed directly up to Central Wharf, followed by the George Peabody, and without loss of time the troops commenced to disembark, this work being finished in less than two hours, when the two vessels left the wharf.

The regiment was drawn up by companies, and arms were stacked and knapsacks unslung, when the men were dismissed, a guard being mounted across the wharf. But, prior to this, a large number of men had run up in town to see their friends, supposing their leave allowed them this privilege, and those who did not take this view of the matter remained on the wharf, where hundreds of their friends went to welcome them home.

Soon after the men landed, through the forethought and liberality of Messrs. S. J. Whall and L. M. Dyer, the men were supplied with excellent hot coffee and bread and butter, and thanks to these gentlemen were in every soldier's mouth.

A pleasant incident occurred last evening as the steamer George Peabody, with the left wing of the regiment on board, was passing Fort Warren. The entire garrison turned out and gave continuous cheers of welcome to the returning soldiers, the post band playing "Home, sweet Home." The cheers were returned from the steamer, and were continued until the steamer got a long distance past the fort.

The following is the Roster of the regiment. Several changes have taken place during the term of service of the regiment:

Field and Staff.

Colonel, Francis L. Lee; Lieutenant Colonel, E. C. Cabot; Major, C. W. Dabney, Jr.; Surgeon, T. W. Fisher; Assistant Surgeon, Daniel McPhee; Adjutant, E. C. Johnson; Quartermaster, F. Bush, Jr.; Chaplain E. H. Mall.

Non-Commissioned Staff.—Sergeant Major, Wm. H. Bird; Quartermaster's Sergeant, F. S. Gifford; Commissary's Sergeant, C. D. Woodberry; Hospital Steward, W. C. Brigham; Principal Musician, G. L. Babcock.

Line Officers.

Captains—Company A, J. M. Richardson; B, J. M. Griswold; C, G. B. Lombard; D, H. D. Sullivan; E, S. W. Richardson; F, C. Storrow; G, C. Hunt; H, W. V. Smith; I, J. R. Kendall; K, R. H. Weld.

First Lieutenants—Company A, J. Coffin; B, J. A. Kendrick, Jr.; C, W. Hedge; D, J. H. Blake, Jr.; E, J. S. Newell; F, T. E. Taylor; G, J. C. White; H, A. R. Howe; I, W. D. Hooper; K, F. T. Brown.

Second Lieutenants—Company A, C. G. Kendall; B, C. C. Soule; C, J. W. Briggs; D, A. H. Stebbins; E, J. S. Cumston; F, H. S. Stebbins; G, F. Odiorne; H, J. L. Mulliken; J, B. F. Fields, Jr.; K, J. Parkinson, Jr.

The regiment has been in five engagements, viz.: Rawls' Mills, Kinston, Whitehall, Goldsboro' and Washington, all in North Carolina, in which thirteen men were killed. On leaving Massachusetts there was an aggregate of 1018 in the regiment, and it returns with 916, one hundred and two men having been killed in battle, died from disease or been discharged for disability.

Prior to the departure of the regiment from Newbern, the following order was issued by Major General Foster, which shows how well the men have served their country during their term of service:

Headquarters 18th Army Corps,
Newbern, N.C., June 5th, 1863.
Special Orders No. 160—17.

The Commanding General, on bidding farewell to the 44th Regiment M. V. M. conveys to them his high appreciation of and thanks for their services whilst in this Department.

As a part of the garrison of Washington, and in the various duties to which they have been assigned, they have always done their duty as soldiers.

The Commanding General in parting expresses his hopes to officers and men that he may have the pleasure of welcoming their return here, and tenders them, one and all, his best and kindest wishes for the future.

By command of MAJOR GENERAL J. C. FOSTER.
(Signed) S. Hoffman, A.A. G.

The escort assembled on the Tremont street Mall of the Common, and at 10 o'clock left there for Central Wharf. The companies forming the escort were under command of Major J. Putnam Bradlee, and consisted of the New England Guard Reserve with 93 guns; the Massachusetts Rifle Club, Captain Moore, with 114 guns; the Battalion of National guards, Major C. W. Stevens, with 102 guns, and the Roxbury Reserve Guard, Captain Wyman, with 80 guns; the whole headed by Gilmore's and the Brigade Bands.

On reaching Central wharf the escort was drawn up in line along India street, and the Regiment being formed on the wharf, the usual preliminary proceedings to the taking up the escort were gone through with, and the column moved over the prescribed route to the Common, entering at the gate at the corner of Charles and Beacon streets.

All along the route the streets were crowded to excess, and the windows were filled with ladies, who cheered the men with a will as they marched along. Bouquets were showered on them from every side, and the entire march was an ovation of which the regiment must have felt proud.

After entering the parade ground the regiment marched past the escort and then wheeled into line in front, the right resting on Beacon street mall. The Mayor and City Government were in waiting in front of the regiment, and Colonel Lee having opened his ranks and saluted, brought his men to the "parade rest." His Honor Mayor [Frederic W.] Lincoln then advanced in front of the line, being accompanied by General [Daniel] Tyler, Chairman of the Committee of Arrangements, and addressed Colonel Lee as follows:

Mr. Commander:—In behalf of the Municipal Government and the people of Boston, it is my duty and privilege to extend to you and your command, the 44th Regiment of Massachusetts Volunteers, a cordial and hearty welcome on your return home from the seat of war. The presence of this large assembly, the crowds of citizens who have greeted you in our thronged streets, the eager impatience with which your arrival has been anticipated, is an evidence that this is not merely an official act of common courtesy and form. The peculiar circumstances under which your regiment was organized, the character, education and social position of the young men who compose its rank and file, the alacrity with which they rallied to arms upon the call of the President, last summer, the good order which has distinguished them in the camp, and the valor and gallant deeds which they have shown in the field, have awakened an unusual interest in the community of which they form a part.

It has been said that a nation could not rely for defence, in time of danger, upon the young men brought up in a city. The habits and associations of a metropolitan life it was feared unfitted them for those stern duties and personal physical labors which they must endure in a soldier's career, and which their brothers from the agricultural districts, on account of their accustomed avocations, were better calculated to perform. But the experience of the past two years has conquered that prejudice, if it really ever existed to any considerable extent, for we have found that some of the most gallant achievements of the war have been by those regiments which have hailed from the cities of the land, and from young men whose infancy was cradled in luxury and ease. It is not always the largest in stature, or those whose muscles are the best developed, but it is the spirit in the man which commands success, and the homely virtues of pluck and courage are not confined to particular classes or business pursuits, but exist wherever the true fire of disinterested patriotism inspires the breast.

You went forth to the distant scene of the conflict at a time when you must have had a full knowledge of the dangers which you were to encounter, and the sacrifices you must make, offering up even your lives, if need be, to preserve the liberties of your country. You loved your homes, you were bound by the tenderest ties of affectionate relatives and friends, and because those sentiments were so strong in your breasts you were ready to do, and to dare, anything and everything in their behalf.

The flag of our country which has floated over you has been the symbol of all that makes life dear, and you have defended it with a resolution and manliness which has conferred honor upon yourselves, and added renown to the old Commonwealth under whose auspices you went forth to meet the common enemy.

We owe you a debt of gratitude for what you have done; we know now that we can rely upon you if the occasion should again call for your services. We mourn for the honored dead and would pay our tribute of respect to the memory of your brave comrades who have fallen in battle or who have been struck by disease in the line of their duty, and we would bless the kind Providence which has protected so many to be again united in family circles, and to enjoy the comforts of homes which have been rendered more precious by the sacrifices you have made. In the future you can look back upon the campaign you have past with just pride, and can feel that in this crisis of our nation's history you have acquitted yourselves like men and patriots.

I cannot conclude without acknowledging the important aid given to your regiment in a perilous period in your history by the 5th Rhode Island Regiment, Col. [Henry T.] Sisson, who, I am happy to hear, is present, and can bear to his command the gratitude of our people for their timely assistance.

Having said thus much and congratulated you upon this auspicious occasion, I invite you to the repast which has been prepared and which fair hands are now waiting to serve.

Col. Lee briefly responded, thanking the city authorities for the handsome manner in which the regiment had been received, and expressing the gratification it gave him to be able to bring back so many men. He assured the Mayor that he felt proud of his kind mention of Col. Sisson and the brave 5th Rhode Island Regiment, as his gallant action in the relief of Washington was one of the most noteworthy of the war.

At the close of Col. Lee's response the various companies in the regiment wheeled into platoons and stacked arms, when they were dismissed to partake of the collation, which was spread on separate tables for each company, on the Charles street mall. The tables were tended by ladies, and presented a beautiful appearance from the number of bouquets of flowers adorning them. The Germania Band furnished good music during the time the regiment was partaking of refreshments.

A large crowd assembled on the Common, and after the collation warmly embraced their friends in the regiment.

* * *

At the conclusion of the ceremonies on the Common, the regiment was granted a furlough until the succeeding Monday at sunset, when they were ordered to report at Readville. On the succeeding Thursday, June 18th, we were mustered out of the service of the United States.

NOTES

INTRODUCTION

1. James W. Geary, *We Need Men: The Union Draft in the Civil War* (DeKalb: Northern Illinois University Press, 1991), 10–12, 17. According to Geary, the recent historian of the Civil War draft, the Militia Act established the right of black men to become Union soldiers. Ibid., 29. Few blacks, however, served until Lincoln's Emancipation Proclamation explicitly authorized recruitment.

2. William Schouler, *A History of Massachusetts in the Civil War* (Boston: E. P. Dutton & Co., 1868), 441, 475, 667; *Record of the Service of the Forty-Fourth Massachusetts Volunteer Militia in North Carolina, August 1862 to May 1863* (Boston: Privately printed, 1887), 21. The *Boston Daily Advertiser*, October 16, 1862, reported that the list of draftees "embraced men from all classes of society, rich as well as poor in fair proportions." Because of the fairness of the Massachusetts draft, threatened resistance to it did not materialize. This would not be the case with the Federal draft in 1863. For the enthusiasm with which Bostonians greeted the call for troops during the first part of the war, see Thomas H. O'Connor, *Civil War Boston: Home Front and Battlefield* (Boston: Northeastern University Press, 1997), 102–3.

3. Allan Nevins, James I. Robertson, Jr., and Bell I. Wiley, eds., *Civil War Books: A Critical Bibliography,* 2 vols. (Baton Rouge: Louisiana State University Press, 1967), I, 98. Haines's reports were published as *Letters from the Forty-Fourth Regiment M.V.M.: A Record of the Experience of a Nine Months' Regiment in the Department of North Carolina in 1862–3. By "Corporal"* (Boston: Herald Job Office, 1863).

4. *Massachusetts Soldiers, Sailors, and Marines in the Civil War,* 4 vols. (Norwood,

Mass.: Norwood Press, 1932), IV, 283, 327; *Record of the Service of the Forty-Fourth,* 18, 313.

5. *Record of the Service of the Forty-Fourth,* 22. Readville, ten miles from Boston and three from Dedham, no longer exists as a community.

6. *Boston Daily Advertiser,* August 30, 1862.

7. This statistical profile sharply contrasted with the proportion of farmers in the ranks of the Union army according to Bell I. Wiley's calculations. Wiley concluded that almost one-half of the men in the Union army were farmers, and a far lesser number were clerks. Many were illiterate. *The Life of Billy Yank: The Common Soldier of the Union* (Indianapolis: Bobbs-Merrill Co., 1951), 304–5.

8. Wiley's calculations regarding the ages of Union troops were similar to Haines's statistical profile of his comrades. Most of the men were in their early twenties. Ibid., p. 303. Wiley did not provide data on the political and religious affiliations of the troops.

9. *Boston Herald,* September 25, 1862.

10. *Deacon Samuel Haines of Westbury, Wiltshire, England, and His Descendants in America, 1635–1901* (North Hampton, N.H.: n.p., 1902), 217.

11. "Thanksgiving Address Delivered by A. L. Butler [November 27, 1862]," in DeForest Safford, ed., *The Bay State Forty-Fourth: A Regimental Record* (Boston: Beacon Co., 1863), 14–15. Butler was referring to the early November 1862 raid toward Tarboro, North Carolina. See chapter 4 for an account of this raid. Before his enlistment in the 44th regiment, Butler was clerk of the Cambridge, Massachusetts, Police Court. *Record of the Service of the Forty-Fourth,* 259.

12. The men had been in camp for three weeks before receiving rifles. Prior to joining the army, many of the 44th recruits had never fired a weapon. John J. Wyeth, *Leaves from a Diary while Serving in Co. E, 44th Mass., from September, 1862, to June, 1863* (Boston: L. F. Lawrence & Co., 1878), 9.

13. Colonel Francis L. Lee identified himself as a Newton, Massachusetts, farmer. He had commanded the 4th Massachusetts Militia Battalion before the organization of the 44th regiment and was the brother of Colonel Henry Lee, Jr., a member of Governor Andrew's military staff. He was thirty-nine years of age when the 44th was formed. After the regiment's Federal service, Colonel Lee continued to command the 44th in the state militia. During the postwar period, Lee was active in the regiment's veterans' association, and when he died in 1887 at Westport, New York, the regimental history, then in press, was dedicated to him. *Massachusetts Soldiers in the Civil War,* IV, 271; *Record of the Service of the Forty-Fourth,* 17–18, 319.

14. Wyeth, *Leaves from a Diary,* passim; *Record of the Service of the Forty-Fourth,* 10, 25, 28, 32.

15. *Record of the Service of the Forty-Fourth,* 10, 25, 28, 32.

16. Ibid., 28–29.

17. Wyeth, *Leaves from a Diary*, 11.

18. The spelling of New Bern has varied. Some writers have spelled it New Berne, and at least one contemporary map referred to it as Newberne. Haines wrote it as one word, Newbern. I use the modern spelling, New Bern.

19. Wyeth, *Leaves from a Diary*, 11–12; *Record of the Service of the Forty-Fourth*, 42–44, citing the *Boston Traveller*. The New England Guard was organized in Boston during the War of 1812 to defend the area against the British. It was in no combat operation. After the war, the Guard, consisting "exclusively of gentlemen and men of good moral character," continued its existence, suppressing local disturbances and participating in annual encampments and ceremonies in Boston and other communities. In 1862 the Guard ceased to exist because it reportedly sent "so many of its members into active service that there was not a sufficient number left at home to keep it alive." Some joined the 44th regiment. *Record of the Service of the Forty-Fourth*, 1–10, 20 (quotations).

20. Wyeth, *Leaves from a Diary*, 14.

21. Ibid., 15; Henry Austin Clapp to his mother, October 27, 1862, Henry Austin Clapp Collection, North Carolina Division of Archives and History, Raleigh. In fairness, it should be noted that since the Federal occupation in early 1862, the area between Morehead City and New Bern had been denuded of provisions and stock animals. Many whites had fled to Raleigh and other interior towns, and slaves had sought refuge in New Bern. Oliver S. Coolidge to ?, May 15, 1862, Oliver S. Coolidge Papers, Manuscript Department, Duke University Library, Durham.

22. Wyeth, *Leaves from a Diary*, 15; Henry Austin Clapp to his mother, October 27, 1862, Clapp Collection.

23. A fine account of military operations in eastern North Carolina at this time can be found in John G. Barrett, *The Civil War in North Carolina* (Chapel Hill: University of North Carolina Press, 1963), chapters 5 and 6.

24. General John G. Foster, a native of Whitefield, New Hampshire, attended West Point Military Academy, graduating fourth in the class of 1846. An officer in General Winfield Scott's 1847 campaign against Mexico City, Foster received a severe wound at Molino del Rey. Continuing in the army after the Mexican War, he served as chief engineer for the defenses of Charleston harbor. Foster was at Fort Sumter when it surrendered to the Confederates in April 1861. Later in the year he received an appointment as brigadier general and commanded a brigade in General Burnside's expedition in eastern North Carolina. After replacing Burnside in command, Foster was appointed major general. Until November 1863, he commanded the Department of North Carolina. He later commanded the Army and Department of Ohio and, after suffering severe injuries that resulted from the fall from a horse, commanded minor departments in the South. After the war, Foster served as an officer in the Corps of Engineers. He died in Nashua, New Hampshire, in 1874. Ezra J. Warner,

Generals in Blue: Lives of the Union Commanders (Baton Rouge: Louisiana State University Press, 1964), 157–58; *Record of the Service of the Forty-Fourth,* 61–62.

25. *Record of the Service of the Forty-Fourth,* 56–57.

26. The organizational changes in the Department of North Carolina when the 44th Massachusetts regiment was stationed in the state can be found in *The War of the Rebellion: A Compilation of the Official Records of the Union and Confederate Armies,* 73 vols., 128 parts (Washington, D.C.: Government Printing Office, 1880–1901), ser. I, vol. 18, pp. 468–69, 500–501, 576–77, 736–37 (hereinafter cited as OR).

27. *Record of the Service of the Forty-Fourth,* 53–54; Wyeth, *Leaves from a Diary,* 15; Joseph W. Denny, *Wearing the Blue in the Twenty-fifth Mass. Volunteer Infantry, with Burnside's Coast Division, 8th Army Corps, and Army of the James* (Worcester: Putnam and Davis, 1879), 107–8. Although many whites fled New Bern with the approach of Burnside's army, some returned when they learned that their persons and property would be protected.

28. William C. Harris, *With Charity for All: Lincoln and the Restoration of the Union* (Lexington: University Press of Kentucky, 1997), 69–71.

29. Joe A. Mobley, *James City: A Black Community in North Carolina, 1863–1900* (Raleigh: North Carolina Department of Cultural Resources, Division of Archives and History, 1981), 5, Appendix, Table 1.

30. James S. Humphreys, "The Federal Army in Eastern North Carolina" (M.A. thesis, North Carolina State University, 1989), 24, 26; Henry Austin Clapp to his mother, October 27, 1862, Clapp Collection; Rowland M. Hall to Frances Anne and Elizabeth Prescott Hall, June 13, 1862, Stickney Family Papers, North Carolina Division of Archives and History, Raleigh; Norman Delaney, ed., "Letters of a Maine Soldier Boy," *Civil War History* 5, no. 1 (March 1959): 54–55.

31. Haines estimated the Federal force at 10,000 troops. General John G. Foster in his report of the operation placed the number at 5,000. OR, ser. I, vol. 18, pp. 20–21.

32. See General Foster's report, November 12, 1862, on the battle of Rawle's Mill, in OR, ser. I, vol. 18, pp. 22–23.

33. *Record of the Service of the Forty-Fourth,* 122. This writer indicated that the army's "officers vigorously attempted to restrain" the troops, many of whom had been "made frenzied by apple-jack, which was found in plenty" in Hamilton. Ibid. Apple-jack was brandy distilled from hard cider. In addition to Hamilton, Foster's troops also pillaged in Williamston. Delaney, ed., "Letters of a Maine Soldier Boy," 60.

34. Report of General John G. Foster, November 12, 1862, OR, ser. I, vol. 18, p. 21.

35. Barrett, *The Civil War in North Carolina,* 136, 139; correspondent for the *Boston Transcript,* November 13, 1862, in Frank Moore, ed., *The Rebellion Record: Diary of American Events, with Documents, Narratives, Illustrative Incidents, Poetry, etc.,* 12 vols. (reprint, New York: Arno Press, 1977), 6:194.

36. See also Wyeth, *Leaves from a Diary,* 21–22, for a similar account of the Thanksgiving Day activities of the men of the 44th regiment.

37. Ibid., 23.

38. Ibid., 26; Barrett, *The Civil War in North Carolina,* 139–44.

39. Report of Colonel Thomas G. Stevenson, Second Brigade Commander, December 21, 1862, OR, ser. I, vol. 18, pp. 82–83; Wyeth, *Leaves from a Diary,* 27 (quotation).

40. General John G. Foster to General Henry W. Halleck, December 27, 1862, OR, ser. I, vol. 18, pp. 54–59; *Record of the Service of the Forty-Fourth,* 141–43; Barrett, *The Civil War in North Carolina,* 146–48.

41. Wyeth, *Leaves from a Diary,* 30.

42. General John G. Foster to General Henry W. Halleck, December 20 and December 27, 1862, OR, ser. I, vol. 18, pp. 54, 489.

43. Other soldiers agreed with Haines's assessment of army morale after the failure of the Goldsboro operation. One soldier later wrote that the day the troops returned to New Bern was the "saddest day" he had "seen in the army." Barrett, *The Civil War in North Carolina,* 146–48.

44. Earl J. Hess, *The Union Soldier in Battle: Enduring the Ordeal of Combat* (Lawrence: University Press of Kansas, 1997), 111.

45. For another account of the malaria epidemic, see Wyeth, *Leaves from a Diary,* 32–33.

46. General Lee did not have much confidence in the success of a Confederate campaign to drive the Federal forces from eastern North Carolina, but he agreed to General Hill's attempt because of the need to regain undisputed control of a major source of his army's agricultural provisions. He wrote General James Longstreet, his subordinate and area commander, that the Federals if driven from their position "can easily escape to their gunboats" and return later to the area. General Robert E. Lee to General James Longstreet, March 30, 1863, OR, ser. I, vol. 18, pp. 906–7.

47. Lieutenant Colonel Southard Hoffman, Assistant Adjutant General, Department of North Carolina, to Colonel Francis L. Lee, January 31, 1863; Report of Colonel Francis L. Lee, Forty-Fourth Massachusetts Infantry, February 14, 1863, both in OR, ser. I, vol. 18, pp. 145–48; Lieutenant Commander Charles W. Flusser to Commander A. Murray, February 6, 1863, *Official Records of the Union and Confederate Navies in the War of the Rebellion,* 27 vols. (Washington, D.C.: Government Printing Office, 1894–1917), ser. I, vol. 8, p. 508. Flusser insisted that the expedition attack the Confederate stronghold at Rainbow Bluffs, farther upriver than Williamston. Colonel Lee's orders directed him to clear rebels from the area around Williamston.

48. Report of Colonel Francis L. Lee, Forty-Fourth Massachusetts Infantry, Feb-

ruary 14, 1863, OR, ser. I, vol. 18, pp. 146–47; *Record of the Service of the Forty-Fourth,* 150–54.

49. Wyeth, *Leaves from a Diary,* 39.

50. Several companies of the 44th formed debating clubs, which reportedly "proved quite attractive to many of [the] men." *Record of the Service of the Forty-Fourth,* 106. Of course, sin and troop misconduct were not absent from the Federal army at New Bern. Though General Foster issued strict orders against selling liquor to soldiers and even prohibited troops from visiting the town after dark, violations occurred, particularly among officers and enlisted men of non–New England regiments. *New Bern Progress,* January 31, 1863; Lieutenant Rowland M. Hall of the 3rd New York cavalry to David P. Hall, July 7, 1862; Lieutenant Hall to Caroline H. Hall, August 5, 1862; Lieutenant Hall to Elizabeth Prescott and Frances Anne Hall, February 15, 1863, all in Stickney Family Papers.

51. *New Bern Progress,* January 21, 1863.

52. Barrett, *The Civil War in North Carolina,* 151–55.

53. Colonel Francis L. Lee to Lieutenant Colonel Southard Hoffman, March 23, 1863, OR, ser. I, vol. 18, p. 567.

54. Wyeth, *Leaves from a Diary,* 43; *Record of the Service of the Forty-Fourth,* 164.

55. Wyeth, *Leaves from a Diary,* 44; *Record of the Service of the Forty-Fourth,* 165; Hal Bridges, *Lee's Maverick General: Daniel Harvey Hill* (New York: McGraw-Hill Book Company, 1961), 176.

56. Wyeth, *Leaves from a Diary,* 45–49. An extended account of the siege of Fort Washington, including excerpts from contemporary sources, can be found in *Record of the Service of the Forty-Fourth,* chapter 9. See also General Foster's report to General Henry W. Halleck, April 30, 1863, OR, ser. I, vol. 18, pp. 212–16.

57. Wyeth, *Leaves from a Diary,* 49–50; Barrett, *The Civil War in North Carolina,* 161.

58. Richard Reid, "Raising the African Brigade: Early Black Recruitment in Civil War North Carolina," *North Carolina Historical Review* 70, no. 3 (July 1993): 269; *Record of the Service of the Forty-Fourth,* 262. On Colonel Lee's recommendation, two enlisted men in the 44th received commissions in Colonel Shaw's regiment. Both died in the famous but futile assault on Fort Wagner in Charleston harbor in July 1863. Ibid., 263–64. Another enlisted man, Garth W. James, the brother of Henry and William James, also joined the 54th regiment. James was wounded at Fort Wagner and survived the war. Russell Duncan, ed., *Blue-Eyed Child of Fortune: The Civil War Letters of Colonel Robert Gould Shaw* (Athens and London: University Press of Georgia, 1992), 333–34n.

59. Assistant Adjutant General Thomas M. Vincent to Colonel Edward A. Wild, April 13, 1863, OR, ser. III, vol. 3, p. 122.

60. Reid, "Raising the African Brigade," 268–69, 287–88; Mobley, *James City,* 16–19.

61. Wyeth, *Leaves from a Diary,* 54.

62. Schouler, *A History of Massachusetts in the Civil War,* 474. The *Boston Herald,* June 10, 1863, as cited by Haines, indicated that 916 men returned. The desertions occurred before the troops left Massachusetts.

63. See the table of losses by the Massachusetts regiments in Schouler, *A History of Massachusetts in the Civil War,* 474.

64. Wyeth also described the homecoming festivities. *Leaves from a Diary,* 54. See also *Record of the Service of the Forty-Fourth,* 218–19. Governor Andrew, who was in New York, sent his regrets that he could not attend the homecoming activities.

65. William F. Hanna, "The Boston Draft Riot," *Civil War History* 36, no. 3 (September 1990): 263–68; Schouler, *A History of Massachusetts in the Civil War,* 476–80.

66. *Record of the Service of the Forty-Fourth,* 293–94.

67. Ibid., 270, 272–76.

68. Ibid., 254, 295, 313; *Deacon Samuel Haines,* 217. A search of the Civil War pension index in the National Archives did not locate a file on Haines. Letter to the editor from Walter B. Hill, Jr., of the National Archives, May 20, 1997.

I. AT READVILLE, MASSACHUSETTS

1. Lieutenant S. W. Putnam of the 20th Massachusetts Regiment fell at the battle of Ball's Bluff near Washington on October 21, 1861. Schouler, *A History of Massachusetts in the Civil War,* 234. Federal forces suffered a humiliating defeat in this early encounter with the Confederates. Colonel Edward Baker, an Oregon senator and an old Illinois friend of President Lincoln, was killed in the battle.

2. A Boston clerk, Captain Henry D. Sullivan, the commander of Haines's company, was only twenty-one years of age when the 44th was organized. He was a former officer in the 4th Battalion. Both Lieutenants James H. Blake and Asa H. Stebbins were young Company D officers and residents of Boston. During the 1880s Stebbins engaged in mining in Arizona, living in notorious Tombstone. *Record of the Service of the Forty-Fourth,* 23, 304, 328, 330.

3. Captains Hunt, Lombard, and Kendall commanded other companies in the 44th regiment. All were in their twenties; the oldest, Lombard, was twenty-five. Ibid., 316, 318, 320.

4. This "queenly agent" has not been identified.

5. Dancing.

6. Governor John A. Andrew was the commander-in-chief of the Massachusetts regiments. Brigadier General Richard A. Peirce commanded the Readville camp.

Andrew's no-bathing order was issued after officials of the Boston and Providence Railroad complained of the activity. *Record of the Service of the Forty-Fourth,* 29.

7. In Greek mythology, a naiad was a nymph presiding over brooks, springs, and fountains. In Roman history, the wife of Julius Caesar supposedly was above reproach in her conduct.

8. Captain James Richardson commanded Company A.

9. Charles Adams enlisted from Medford, Massachusetts, not North Carolina. *Record of the Service of the Forty-Fourth,* 302.

10. Facings are turning movements by soldiers in order to face in a given direction.

11. Sparrowgrass was the main character in Frederick S. Cozzens, *The Sparrowgrass Papers* (1856).

12. A meerschaum pipe is a tobacco pipe with a white bowl coated in magnesium silicate. A dudeen is a short-stemmed clay pipe.

13. Sutlers were peddlers who established makeshift stores near camp and sold goods to the troops. As was the case with the sutler who sold to the men of the 44th, many of these peddlers took advantage of the troops and charged high prices for often inferior goods. A "vegetable oyster" is a salsify, a plant whose roots are eaten.

14. Major General Jesse L. Reno was killed in the battle of South Mountain on September 14, 1862. Though not a New Englander, he was buried in Boston, the residence of his wife. Reno, Nevada, was named for him. Warner, *Generals in Blue,* 395.

15. Azure.

16. Lieutenant Colonel Wilder Dwight of Brookline died of wounds suffered in the battle of Antietam on September 17. His funeral was virtually a state affair, with Governor Andrew and other Massachusetts dignitaries in attendance. Justin Winsor, ed., *The Memorial History of Boston,* 4 vols. (Boston: James R. Osgood and Co., 1881), III: 322n; *Boston Daily Advertiser,* September 26, 1862.

17. On October 6, 1862, Charles C. Soule enlisted as a private in Company F. Three weeks later Soule, only twenty years of age, received a commission as a second lieutenant in Company B. *Record of the Service of the Forty-Fourth,* 284, 329.

18. There were nine Smiths in the regiment. This Smith has not been identified.

19. Indeed, Colonel Thomas G. Stevenson was placed in command of the brigade but was not promoted to brigadier general until November. He died on May 10, 1864, in the bloody battle of Spotsylvania. Even before his heroic death, Stevenson had become one of New England's most respected generals. *Record of the Service of the Forty-Fourth,* 63.

20. The Joseph Short Patent Knapsack was a two-piece knapsack of black enamelled canvas, attached by a four-inch rigid strap at the top. Manufactured in Salem, Massachusetts, this knapsack was kept in position by two short arms on each side of the waist, thus avoiding the use of any straps across the chest. Designed for comfort,

it was popular with Massachusetts troops, as Haines suggests. The U.S. Army Regulation Double-Bag Knapsack, issued by the government, was not as comfortable as the Short Knapsack. Frederick P. Todd, *American Military Equipage, 1851–1872* (Westbrook, Conn.: The Company of Military Historians, 1974; reprint New York: Charles Scribner's Sons, 1980), 206, 208.

21. This refers to Lincoln's preliminary Emancipation Proclamation issued on September 22, 1862.

22. These were Boston firms.

23. The United States Sanitary Commission was a voluntary organization designed to shape medical and hygienic conditions in the Federal army. It proved its worth, despite the opposition of the Army Medical Bureau. By 1863, 7,000 local affiliates existed in the North, with tens of thousands of volunteer workers, mainly women, providing assistance to the men in the field. James M. McPherson, *Battle Cry of Freedom: The Civil War Era* (Oxford: Oxford University Press, 1988), 480–82.

24. Brobdingnag was a country in Jonathan Swift's *Gulliver's Travels* where all the people were gigantic.

2. EN ROUTE TO NEW BERN, NORTH CAROLINA

1. Mr. Pickwick, known for his good-heartedness, was the hero of Charles Dickens's *The Pickwick Papers*.

2. Mark Tapley was the servant of Martin Chuzzlewit in Charles Dickens's novel *Martin Chuzzlewit*. Tapley was known for his virtue, irrepressible jollity, and optimism. Dickens seems to have been Haines's favorite author.

3. NEW BERN

1. See note 2, chapter 2.

2. "Contrabands" was the name given to blacks entering Federal lines by General Benjamin F. Butler in early 1862 when his troops occupied the Norfolk area. Butler referred to these slaves as contraband of war and, in effect, proceeded to free them. For the remainder of the war, Union soldiers routinely referred to ex-slaves in the occupied areas as "contraband."

3. Zouaves were Civil War military units characterized by colorful uniforms and precision drilling. They were patterned after French infantry troops composed of Algerian recruits.

4. Swansboro was a village on Bogue Inlet, about fifty miles north of Wilmington. It was the northernmost Confederate outpost on the Atlantic coast.

4. THE TARBORO EXPEDITION

1. Haines, using uncharacteristically strong language in referring to Washington, North Carolina, as a "bastard" town, probably had in mind the town's strong support

for the rebellion, despite its early opposition to secession immediately after Lincoln's election.

2. A hoe-cake was a Southern cake made of cornmeal, water, and salt, baked before a fire or in the ashes. It was so-called because it was originally cooked on a hoe.

3. In the February 28, 1861, state election rejecting the meeting of a state convention that might have taken North Carolina out of the Union, Beaufort County (Washington) voted against it. After Fort Sumter and Lincoln's proclamation calling for troops to suppress the Southern insurrection, the town overwhelmingly supported secession.

4. Sugar-box shooks were pieces of wood for assembling boxes to transport sugarcane.

5. This action began the battle of Rawle's Mill.

6. The battles of Roanoke Island (February 7–8, 1862) and New Bern (March 13–14, 1862), prior to the arrival of the 44th Massachusetts regiment, were Union victories that enabled the Federal forces to occupy much of eastern North Carolina.

7. General John A. Dix, a former U.S. Senator from New York and briefly Secretary of Treasury in the administration of President James Buchanan, commanded Federal forces in occupied eastern Virginia in late 1862. General George B. McClellan, unbeknown to Haines, on November 7 had been removed from command of the Army of the Potomac.

8. The black village evidently was on a plantation whose owner had fled. Many planters, however, had managed to take their slaves with them well in advance of the Federal raid.

9. Haines is referring to his own company commander, Captain Henry D. Sullivan.

10. Cocky and relieved after experiencing his first combat, Haines sarcastically labeled the Federal troops defending New Bern as the "Home Guard." Actually, many, if not most of them, had participated in General Burnside's operation to take eastern North Carolina.

11. Captain James Belger's Rhode Island artillery battery played an important role in all of General Foster's 1862 operations in North Carolina. See Moore, ed., *Rebellion Record*, VI: 191, 259, 264.

12. There might have been some substance in the report of Confederate ironclad construction on the Roanoke River. During the spring of 1863 the Confederates began work above Hamilton on the ironclad *Albemarle,* which, when completed in early 1864, temporarily swept Federal gunboats from the Roanoke and made possible the rebel army's victory in the battle of Plymouth. John G. Barrett, *The Civil War in North Carolina* (Chapel Hill: University of North Carolina Press, 1963), 214, 217–20.

13. Haines is referring to a locked chest or cupboard containing the delicacies.

14. A much-ridiculed army issue, hard tack was a hard biscuit or bread made only with unleavened flour and water and without salt, which could be preserved for troops on the march.

15. Weeds was a mourning garment.

16. Asa Biggs, a former U.S. congressman, served as a Confederate district judge during the war.

17. The Newton company was Company B.

18. Salt horse was slang for salted beef.

19. Among his several attributes, Apollo was the god of music; Terpsichore the muse of dancing and choral music.

20. The Hardee refers to the book on military tactics written by Major William J. Hardee and published by the War Department in 1855. It became the bible on tactics for both armies during the Civil War. Ironically, Hardee became a major general in the Confederate army. Patricia L. Faust, ed., *Historical Times Illustrated Encyclopedia of the Civil War* (New York: Harper & Row, 1986), 338–39.

21. Antiques and Horribles were elderly veterans of the New England Guard who frequently paraded in Boston.

5. THE GOLDSBORO CAMPAIGN

1. Actually, the distance of the march was about 120 miles.

2. Foster's army consisted of approximately 11,000 men, not the 15,000 that Haines estimated. Barrett, *The Civil War in North Carolina,* 139.

3. Haines exaggerated the size of Kinston. The town was not large; its population was slightly more than 1,000 in 1860.

4. Peninsula soldiers were troops who were transferred from General McClellan's army to New Bern after fighting in the Peninsula campaign near Richmond.

5. General Nathan G. Evans, the Confederate commander, had only four infantry regiments and a few artillery batteries to resist Foster's force of approximately 11,000 men. Barrett, *The Civil War in North Carolina,* 140–42.

6. The phrase "a Roland for an Oliver" meant a blow for a blow. It alludes to a drawn combat between Roland, the romantic hero of early France, and Oliver, his antagonist.

7. "Old Stars" was the astronomer Horace P. Tuttle of Haines's company.

8. These are casualties for the 44th regiment only. General Foster's report on the Goldsboro expedition gives combined casualty figures for the three battles in the operation (Kinston, Whitehall, and Goldsboro). The 44th suffered eight killed and thirteen wounded, which was the eighth highest of the twenty-five units engaged in the action. The total number of Federals killed, wounded, and missing in the Goldsboro operation was 591. Return of Casualties in the Union Forces, OR, ser. I, vol. 18, p. 60.

1. For the reorganization of the Federal forces in North Carolina, see the Introduction, pp. 11–12.

2. Haines is referring to the nine-month New England troops, commanded by General Nathaniel P. Banks, that were sent to New Orleans to aid in clearing the lower Mississippi River of Confederate forces. Some of these troops were deployed in the ill-fated expedition to take Galveston and speed the work of reconstruction in Texas. Harris, *With Charity for All*, 91–92.

3. Published as *The Bay State Forty-Fourth: A Regimental Record* (Boston: Beacon, 1863).

4. Unidentified. Evidently, Jenkins was a Boston theater critic.

5. Hebes was the goddess who, it was believed, had the power for restoring youth.

6. The U.S. Sanitary Commission had an office in New Bern. The doctors had spirituous drink to treat the wounded.

7. Clash's Hall was an entertainment center in Boston. Matutinal bugle-call refers to early morning sick call.

8. Salt horse was salted beef.

9. Evidently the "lady of color" was a soldier of the 44th regiment with black makeup similar to that of minstrel troupes.

10. Leigh Hunt was a prolific English man of letters who died in 1859. Although Hunt was a brilliant essayist, his reputation was dramatically diminished after his death.

11. Coverings.

12. The *Fry* was a schooner that made the run from Boston to New Bern.

13. General Stevenson survived the battle of Whitehall, only to be killed at Spotsylvania, Virginia, in 1864.

14. "Goff, the Regicide," was William C. Goff of Company D.

15. The road south to Washington, North Carolina.

16. Barnard, Thompson, and Lothrop were Unitarian ministers.

17. For the reports of the two opposing commanders in this engagement, see OR, ser. I, vol. 18, pp. 192–95 (Confederate) and pp. 183–84 (Union). Both reports generally confirm Haines's account.

18. Only officers could bring their families to camp, provided they could obtain living quarters for them. The families of most officers remained in the North. Even those wives who came to North Carolina remained only for a brief period. A few Northern women in New Bern served in the U.S. Sanitary Commission. During the latter part of the war, Northern school teachers arrived in the Federal-occupied towns of eastern North Carolina.

1. In his report, General J. Johnston Pettigrew does not indicate the number of men in his force; however, Haines's figure of 700 Confederates actually engaged in the fight seems reasonable. The report of 8,000 rebels moving down the Trent Road to attack is an exaggeration. Report of General J. Johnston Pettigrew, March 17, 1863, OR, ser. I, vol. 18, pp. 192–95.

2. David Hunter Strother visited the Southern states before the war and, under the pseudonym Porte Crayon, wrote a series of articles, largely anecdotal, regarding the scenes and people he encountered. In 1856 he briefly visited Washington, North Carolina, and described the town, mentioning "a private residence, at the end of the main street, with beautifully-improved grounds." This house could have been Grist's. Strother's sketches have been compiled and published in a book entitled *The Old South Illustrated,* edited and with an introduction by Cecil D. Eby, Jr. (Chapel Hill: University of North Carolina Press, 1959). See page 195 for Strother's description of Washington.

3. Aunt Fanny and family were slaves.

4. Sergeant David K. Hobart, wounded and captured at Washington, died on April 14 at a Confederate hospital in Wilson, North Carolina. Theodore Lawrence and John Leonard became prisoners of war. Though wounded, John King survived and remained with the 44th regiment. *Record of the Service of the Forty-Fourth,* 314, 318.

5. Whitworth guns, developed by Sir Joseph Whitworth of Manchester, England, fired long-range rifled artillery projectiles cast in hexagon form and then precision finished to make the shells slightly concave. Thomas S. Dickey and Peter C. George, *Field Artillery Projectiles of the American Civil War,* 2 vols. (Mechanicsburg, Va.: Arsenal Publications, 1993), 322.

6. Videttes were sentinels stationed outside the fort.

7. The comment regarding "rebel justice" reflected not only the normal hostility of soldiers toward the enemy but also, in Haines's case, a New Englander's prejudiced impression of the South. The man hanged by the Confederates was probably a deserter who had been captured trying to flee to Federal lines. Like Southerners, Northerners also occasionally executed deserters as an example for all to see.

8. The Extinguisher 20 and the boys of Cataract 11 analogy has not been identified.

9. "Cucumbers" were the large shells fired by the Whitworth cannons, one of the largest artillery pieces in the Confederate arsenal.

10. The rumor was correct. A relief force had been repulsed midway between New Bern and Washington. See Introduction, p. 25.

11. George W. Hight's sketch of the defenses at Washington was not printed and has not been found. Solon M. Allis of the 21st Massachusetts regiment also drew a

map of the fortifications and surrounding area. This map was printed in Wyeth, *Leaves from a Diary*, 45.

12. A Maying party refers to a group gathering of flowers in the spring, usually in May.

13. The Department of the South, commanded by General David Hunter, included the South Atlantic coast of South Carolina, Georgia, and Florida.

8. PROVOST DUTY

1. The 54th Massachusetts Regiment was the first black regiment to be organized; it obtained several volunteers from the 44th to serve as officers. The 54th Massachusetts was made famous by the 1989 movie *Glory*.

2. Haines was probably referring to General Joseph Hooker's testimony before the congressional Joint Committee on the Conduct of the War regarding the defeat of General Ambrose E. Burnside's Army of the Potomac at Fredericksburg in December 1862 and its subsequent attempt to flank Lee's army, culminating in the embarrassing "Mud March" of early 1863 along the Rappahannock River.

3. The bloody Sepoy rebellion occurred in India in 1857.

4. The Federal force in the Kinston operation suffered two killed (including Colonel Jones), five wounded, and one missing. Confederate deaths were not reported; General Foster indicated that 165 prisoners had been taken. General John G. Foster to General Henry W. Halleck, June 2, 1863, OR, ser. III, vol. 3, pp. 363–64.

5. Edward Everett and Robert C. Winthrop were prominent Bostonians.

6. There is no evidence that Haines's light-hearted proposal to deliver lectures on the war came to fruition.

9. RETURN TO BOSTON

1. The correct quotation from Wordsworth's "The World Is Too Much with Us" is "Or hear old Triton blow his wreathed horn."

2. Haines was comparing the huge blue sky to the amount of blue cloth required to make a pair of Dutchman's breeches.

BIBLIOGRAPHY

The following are relevant secondary works consulted for this book.

Barrett, John G. *The Civil War in North Carolina.* Chapel Hill: University of North Carolina Press, 1963.

Bridges, Hal. *Lee's Maverick General: Daniel Harvey Hill.* New York: McGraw-Hill Book Company, 1961.

Geary, James W. *We Need Men: The Union Draft in the Civil War.* DeKalb: Northern Illinois University Press, 1991.

Hanna, William F. "The Boston Draft Riot." *Civil War History* 36, no. 3 (September 1990): 262–73.

Harris, William C. *With Charity for All: Lincoln and the Restoration of the Union.* Lexington: University Press of Kentucky, 1997.

Hess, Earl J. *The Union Soldier in Battle: Enduring the Ordeal of Combat.* Lawrence: University Press of Kansas, 1997.

Humphreys, James S. "The Federal Army in Eastern North Carolina." M.A. thesis, North Carolina State University, 1989.

McPherson, James M. *For Cause and Comrades: Why Men Fought in the Civil War.* New York and Oxford: Oxford University Press, 1997.

Massachusetts Soldiers, Sailors, and Marines in the Civil War. 4 vols. Norwood, Mass.: Norwood Press, 1932.

Mitchell, Reid. *Civil War Soldiers: Their Expectations and Their Experiences.* New York: Viking Penguin, Inc., 1988.

Mobley, Joe A. *James City: A Black Community in North Carolina, 1863–1900.* Raleigh:

North Carolina Department of Cultural Resources, Division of Archives and History, 1981.

Moore, Frank, ed. *The Rebellion Record: Diary of American Events, with Documents, Narratives, Illustrative Incidents, Poetry, etc.* 12 vols. Reprint, New York: Arno Press, 1977.

O'Connor, Thomas H. *Civil War Boston: Home Front and Battlefield.* Boston: Northeastern University Press, 1997.

Record of the Service of the Forty-Fourth Massachusetts Volunteer Militia in North Carolina, August 1862 to May 1863. Boston: Privately printed, 1887.

Reid, Richard. "Raising the African Brigade: Early Black Recruitment in Civil War North Carolina." *North Carolina Historical Review* 70, no. 3 (July 1993): 266–99.

Robertson, James I., Jr. *Soldiers Blue and Gray.* Columbia: University of South Carolina Press, 1988.

Schouler, William. *A History of Massachusetts in the Civil War.* Boston: E. P. Dutton & Co., 1868.

Warner, Ezra J. *Generals in Blue: Lives of the Union Commanders.* Baton Rouge: Louisiana State University Press, 1964.

Welcher, Frank J. *The Union Army, 1861–1865: Organization and Operations.* Vol. 1, *The Eastern Theater.* Bloomington and Indianapolis: Indiana University Press, 1989.

INDEX